FARTHER ON

FARTHER ON

*A true story challenging those who doubt
and encouraging those who believe.*

KAREN GRYDER WITH SANDY FAULKNER

WestBow
PRESS
A DIVISION OF THOMAS NELSON

WestBow Press books may be ordered through booksellers or by contacting:

WestBow Press
A Division of Thomas Nelson
1663 Liberty Drive
Bloomington, IN 47403
www.westbowpress.com
1-(866) 928-1240

ISBN: 978-1-4497-2442-9 (sc)
ISBN: 978-1-4497-2443-6 (hc)
ISBN: 978-1-4497-3211-0 (e)

Library of Congress Control Number: 2011961165

Printed in the United States of America

WestBow Press rev. date: 12/16/2011

Prepare for a journey into isolated, back woods Appalachia, colored by the poverty and abuse possible in that environment. Watch for the impact of those who ignore a child's desparation compared to the impact of a few wonderful individuals daring to give this pitiful child encouragement to survive—even though at times their sensitivity came in something as small as a milk carton.

Karen's gratitude to have survived an amazingly awful past filters into her story. Her transparency allows you to share her desire to be an advocate and voice for children who are hungry, neglected, domestically abused, or unprepared for pregnancy. You will be compelled to share in what has become her passion and purpose in life.

Karen Gryder shares her amazing faith and perseverence during poverrty, abuse and neglect. Sandy Faulkner is blessed by the opportunity to write and edit Karen's story. It is an honor to call Karen 'friend'.

A Dedication

by KAREN GRYDER

I dedicate my part of *Farther On* to my precious children Kristina Marie Bell, Johnathan Andrew Bell and Eva Grace Gryder. The three of you bring immeasurable joy to my life. I am forever grateful for each one of you.

TABLE OF CONTENTS

Perspectives

PREFACE

My Grateful Heart

My heart might explode without a chance to tell my story. Gettin' to talk about the hard times kinda' lessens the power those trials have over me. But, most of all I especially need a chance to share how God has used a lot of people in my life to bring me through each bad day. So, if you reached out to me in the form of food, shelter, clothing, encouragement or prayer, My Heavenly Father saw each act of kindness and I want you to know, HE *will* bless you for it.

I rest assured HE will bless the families (Boyds, Byrds, and Moores) for finding room in their hearts and homes to accept me as though I was their own. Each of my siblings (Lona Stiltner, Lilly Mai Byers, Mary Stacy, Teressa White, Melissa Burkes, James Coleman, Ray Coleman and Rose Hall)—will be counted as a gift. It is a privilege to be numbered among each brother and sister and to know their unique stories.

Without Brad, my husband, supplying patience, understanding, and love, I might have remained silent when others said, "You *have* to share your story." Plus, church friends like Dale Faulkner pushed me on with encouragement while Sandy Faulkner shared compassion, perseverance and typing skills to make my story come alive today. 'Cause of them I can share my passion: to be a voice for children hurtin' cause of hunger, neglect, and domestic abuse.

I want others to notice, and not ignore children's needs. I want people to understand that growin' up in emotional and physical poverty leads to scared young people who ain't prepared to change the circumstances of the life they inherit. I especially want to be sure to talk to young girls, clear and direct, to support them if, cause of seekin love and support, they end up pregnant and unprepared to provide for their own children. I want these girls to know that with the help of God and his servants, they can make it through and their children deserve a life—one that's better than what they was offered. I want to say that life is like a journey that we all have to take and we all need each other. Gettin' to say these things is my passion and my purpose in life.

ACKNOWLEDGMENTS

Following Sunday School less than a year ago at Luby's Cafeteria in
Houston, Texas Karen and Sandy talked about sharing Karen's story.
Without the encouragement of caring people, gifted professionals,
and the faith-filled lessons of many, the project would surely remain
undone. Despite beginning with insecurity, we humbly believed God
was orchestrating the project and pushing us to finish, regardless of
the outcome. HE placed resources in our lives including:

AMANDA EARP – Graphic Designer
ROBBY GREEN – Graphic Design Advisor
WESTBOW PUBLISHING
DR. JAMES DOBSON – Psychologist and Theologian
ELIZABETH ELLIOTT – MISSIONARY and Author
BETH MOORE – Author and Bible Study Leader
CAROLE LEWIS – Author and Director of "First Place"
RUTHANNE MEFFORD – Executive Director, Child Advocates
of Fort Bend

Individuals at Houston's First Baptist Church who continue to
encourage us with lessons of faith and examples of fellowship:

Pastor – Gregg Matte
First Place Director, Author – Carole Lewis
'His Glory' Sunday School Class Teachers and Members

We thank God for each need HE's met using others!

PROLOGUE

Well, even as bad as home was,
we always wanted to go back there
'cause we knew we belonged there.

My name is Karen Gryder. First, I want to say that I ain't no movie star. I ain't never invented anything or achieved anything great. In other words, I don't have no claim to fame. I grew up thinkin' I was worthless and dead weight on society—what folks might call "poor white trash." Now I'm convinced I'm one of a kind, highly valued, and highly favored—at least by my Father, the King. Yeah! I forgot to mention my Father, the King. This is how I got from livin' in a two-room shack in despair to livin' a life with so much happiness and joy that I can hardly stand it. These days I often start by sayin', "Thank you, Jesus, for a floor under my feet, food to eat, a family to love, and all my blessings." While grocery shoppin' I slip into thinkin' *it must be Christmas—I can get what I want and what I need.* Seems crazy but when someone I don't know too well asks, just to be polite, "how are you today?", I quick as ever say, "I'm smilin' so big I've got lipstick on my ears!"

I was born Karen Coleman in a tiny Virginia coal mining town in thick backwoods that had so many treetops coverin' them hills, they looked like a thick green, gorgeous blanket. Bein' number seven of twelve children had its pluses and minuses. My daddy was a coal miner. These are my memories and mine alone; the other children likely seen things different, but one thing for sure, these happenin's are the truth to me 'bout my past.

For I reckon that the sufferings of this present time are not worthy to be compared with the glory which shall be revealed in us. (Rom. 8:18)

Sharon

My first memories are of bein' with my twin sister, Sharon. I 'magine we was 'round two years old, 'cause she was still there. I remember sittin'—well, really, I remember little glimpses of playin' with her. We'd be hangin' out together in the center of what I used to call our two-room shack. Well, just lately, I found out the shack was really a barn made with crooked, splintered pine plank walls havin' holes so big you could see the outside. In fact, some of 'em was big enough to poke stuff through. Not sure the barn was meant to be a home, 'cause it only had a tiny workin' table in one corner and that was our "kitchen." One washbasin, one drinkin' water bucket with dipper, and two red rusty coal buckets sittin' next to the stove—that was our "house." Havin' so many kids, there was beds everywhere, including the kitchen, 'cause there weren't much room and no walls for privacy.

So, in my mind, the picture's purty clear: Sharon and I'd be plopped down, legs straight out, right next to each other near that workin' table. Not havin' much furniture, we'd just sit on the dirt floor, which smelled kinda musty, moldy, and damp; it felt, well, the soil it felt hard, like cold concrete. It always felt cool on my bottom. When we would eat, we'd sit close enough to be sharin' and eatin' with our fingers. Truth is, I remember sometimes grabbin' food from her side of the plate—seems like hers always looked lots better'n mine. I can still see Sharon—she was 'bout two years old.

When the barn door was open midday, the sun shined through just right, catchin' her hair from behind, makin' it look the same color as sourwood honey. She was tiny and frail, but she was beautiful.

One day without any warnin', Sharon just disappeared from our lives. I'm not sure if it was somethin' we ever used, but there was a small wishin' well, probably just built for decoration, at ground level. Its wall was not real tall, and it'd been carefully made from flat natural mountain stones red-rich with iron; they was all stacked together real tight. The well sat in the front yard next to the rock path leadin' away from the house we was rentin'. Since it held a little water, our landlord used it for keeping his minners for fishin'. We was always thinkin' to be careful to keep it covered most times.

Everyone said the bigger kids, they'd been stickin' their feet in the cool well water on that hot, humid summer day. Daddy took off with the older siblin's up the road to an aunt's house. Mama said me and Sharon, we was playin' on a quilt she'd spread out on the porch real neat, all the while tellin us, "You two stay put." She was tryin' to get the never-endin' pile of laundry done on our old ringer washer—the kind you had to feed the clothes through piece by piece—and she was sayin, "gimme 'bout twenty more minutes 'n I'll be done." Somehow Sharon must have run off, and mama couldn't find her nowhere. My mama was a good mama, but as anyone with kids knows, you turn your back one split second, and they'll be gone 'fore you turn around and blink twice. So we went lookin' high and low.

Anyway, Mama said I came tuggin' at her dress and drug her over to the well; she looked in and she let out a holler. Mama stood still in shock a minute 'cause all she could see were Sharon's feet stickin' up. Bein' a tiny woman, she had to stretch, lean, and struggle hard to get Sharon out, pullin' up on her feet with all she had. Sharon's limp body finally reached the top of the well wall, and then her listless little body kinda fell forward into my precious mama's tiny arms, almost causin' her to fall backwards. Strainin' with all her might, she got her balance enough to, in a panic, start runnin' up the road—bawlin' and clutchin' onto her little one's lifeless form with me, another little two-year-old, runnin' and hollerin' close behind her. Mama was yellin' and frantic lookin' for anyone who could help. A coal miner stopped and chased my mama down tryin' to do CPR, but it was too late.

Sharon died in his arms, and it touched him so deeply that his company and all his co-workers sent flowers. It's been said that Sharon had more flowers than anyone had ever seen in our little town. My family was so poor that we couldn't get nothin' for her, but she had plenty, thanks to the stranger who took time to stop and help Mama in her desperate time of need.

God caused this man to stop, I just know it. There ain't no real purpose for flowers and they don't last, but weren't it nice that Sharon had so many sent to remember her? Plus them flowers, they all came with a card, and my mama she held those cards and saved each one o' them. Until her eyesight failed, she'd most often go through the cards, one by one, and see the nice things people had done said. Long after she couldn't read anymore, she'd get her family to read those cards to her as often as they was willin'.

My mama had always talked 'bout getting Sharon and me some twin-like dresses, but we never had money for such. Someone knowin' my mama's heart's wish, well, for the funeral, someone brought over Sharon and me matchin' dresses so that, just this one time, we'd be wearin' purty lookalike clothes. How sad it was for Mama to see her Sharon in the casket and to see me, her twin sister bein' free, runnin', and so full of life. In the funeral picture a family member shared with us, I see Sharon, me, and my mama—her face was just filled with anguish.

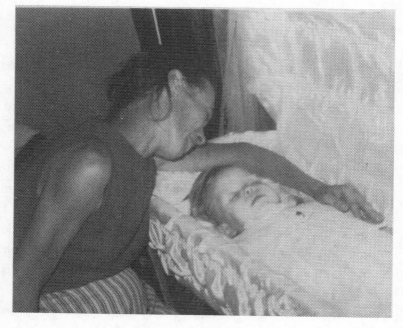

My precious Mama at Sharon's funeral—full of anguish

I don't remember it well, but they say my mama wanted to die. This day just 'bout broke her heart. The other brothers and sisters said Mama changed that day and that she never was the same. Before the funeral someone brought all us kids into the livin' room where mam was and where they had Sharon layin' on the floor; she was covered with a sheet. After we was all sittin' in one spot, they uncovered Sharon so we could see her. Well, I know they was tryin' to help us accept things, and I think maybe it helped us kids, but maybe it didn't. My mama, she started just starin' off into empty space right then, and lots o' times. Truth is, I think it was just too much to look face-to-face at a lifeless Sharon layin' there, right where she'd been playin' the day before.

Pickin' up the Pieces

My mama was desperate with sadness when her precious Sharon died. I can't even imagine what that was like. I think that my daddy—well, really, I'm sure—blamed my mama. One thing was for sure—the neighbors blamed her. They was just those kind o' people. Of course, there was no counseling, 'cause we was so poor. Mama never had any help of any kind. In fact, she never even had friends, 'cause she had all these children, and that meant she never had time for friends. Truth is, she had no time for anythin' fun. I don't know how she survived. She did carry on, but after that day, I think it was without her sanity. Like my siblin's always said, her child's death was when maybe most of the mind changes started takin' place with my mama.

I may not have been 'round at the time, but 'cause of what I saw and what others told me, I knew my daddy was a total drunk. Folks said it was after he and Mama got married that he real quick took to drinkin', and he didn't never give it up. Where we come from, 'bout twenty to thirty years ago, people, they'd spend time at home, havin' fun with music and moonshine. Every outdoor gatherin', we'd be always makin' a small fire out of old, dirty rags. They threw off lots of smoke, which was supposed to keep the mosquitoes down. We'd help make our "gnat fire" most every night, and we'd put it right close to the porch. I can still remember the daily routine of us sittin' there, smellin' that smoke, listenin' to grown-up stories, and watchin' the grown-ups doin' what seemed normal for spendin' their free time. We could tell they was feelin' deservin' 'cause they done worked really hard all day.

It was relaxin' for them to get home, start tellin' stories and makin' music. Most everyone could play some kind of instrument and each one believed they could sing good, 'specially after they started their drinkin'. So this is exactly what my daddy did with all his kin people most every night. He never thought 'bout learnin' how to notice—much less love—his family. I always thought it'd be natural in most people—lovin' their wife and kids—but maybe the alcohol ate away who he was. I'll never understand or know for sure. Regardless, he kept hisself happy just bein' really abusive and actin' like a poor excuse for a daddy—and a poor excuse for a husband. I sure wish someone had helped make him wanna' change sometime durin' our lives, but no one ever tried—not one person tried. It's so sad!

James and Ray

Well, I don't know why, but I can't remember his birth—but I do remember my beautiful, beloved brother James as he was growing up. 'Specially in my mind is him swallowin' a screw, a penny, and a latch pin all at the same time when he was a toddler. That was a scary time for our family. Three things are clear in my mind about that day: we was feelin' scared for him, we was feelin' really poor, and we was feelin' really hungry. The doctor was sayin' not to worry too much and to give James stuff that was soft.

'Cause my mama wasn't educated and not very smart, she decided to give James instant mashed potatoes—the kind of powdered stuff that came in the box. Us kids never got them before, 'cause they was way too expensive. We watched my mama mix the powder with hot water, and that stuff smelled so good, our mouths was waterin'. That's what she gave James. Finally, he did pass all that stuff he done swallowed. I remember feelin' jealous, 'cause James got to eat those fancy mashed potatoes. For a while, I thought about swallowin' somethin' bad myself, 'cause my stomach was always filled with the pain of hunger!

Next, I remember the birth of my brother Ray, and when mama brought him home. Gettin' ready for him, we had some furniture all set aside. There was a big, brown, worn nylon chair in the livin' room with some large arms—in fact, they were huge—and stuffin' was pokin' out at some spots. In other spots, the fabric was so worn-out, I remember seein' clear down inside them springs. See, we never had the luxury of furniture of any kind—specially no cribs or baby stuff. My mama came home and laid Ray in that chair between those gigantic arms, and he just slept there a lot of the time with a special light blue blanket on him. Every time my mama had a baby, she called a family meetin' to pick one of us kids to watch over the new baby. When Ray was born, she picked me, so Ray became my constant concern when I was only five or six.

No wonder I had a special bond with Ray; I sometimes still consider him mine. He was the most beautiful little boy with the curliest, blondest hair you ever saw. We was always sayin' he was way too purty to be a boy. Mama and Daddy named him Curley Ray Cline Coleman, and that name caused him lots of problems. When he got older, he was so picked on that we all decided to just call him Ray. To this day, it still causes him pain when someone calls him his given name. 'Curley' may have worked well for the bluegrass singer guy who recorded my daddy's favorite music, but the name sure never worked well for Ray. He *hated and will always hate* his name!

Family Life

Goin' back, I remember when Ray was still just a tiny baby. Our family was always gettin' real sick, and we was real poor. My mama tried to nurse each of us, but she was so malnourished, she didn't have no milk. She'd just mash up any food we had with her fingers and put it in the young'uns' mouths. Even a one-week-old infant would go straight home from the hospital and be eatin' whatever we had. Having no milk, Mama would most times feed her babies "water gravy" or "cornmeal mush," which was flour or meal mixed with water. We survived without any formula or baby food.

Once in a while, we had powdered milk from the giveaway food program (government surplus). That was a real blessin' and the best thing ever! The problem was that them giveaways wasn't too often—maybe once every two to three months. Plus, to get the stuff, we had to be at the post office real early, get in line, and stand in the hot, humid midday sun, waitin' and hopin' we'd get to the front 'fore they ran out. I remember one day, we got lucky 'n' came home with a big brown cardboard surplus box; it was just sittin' on our floor. When everyone was not lookin', I snatched a bag of prunes, went off and hid, and ate the whole dang bag. 'Course, I got sick, but the worst thing was that I felt real bad about stealing it all. I lived and learned, and I do feel sorry 'bout things I did. I was just feelin' desperate with hunger. Most times, we couldn't get no extra food, and I just know my lovin' God took up the difference 'tween the nutrition we got and what we needed; otherwise, we'd be dead.

All these times, my daddy was neglectin' us and actin' angry, mean, and abusive. He'd work the coal mines, plus he was a taxicab driver. I know he didn't make much money off the cab, 'cause we lived in such a small town, and there weren't many people goin' much. At times when town folk did need a ride somewhere, neighbors would help them out 'stead of anyone forkin' out cash. Everybody knew that Daddy drove a cab, and that at any given time, he'd be willin' to offer each of the town's whores a free ride, 'cause he loved women almost as much as he loved booze. He never made much money for us. Many of the women he hauled around lived only two or three houses away from us. I learned to hate these women, 'cause I knew they was takin' bread from our mouths. That's what my mama told us when I was 'bout four or five. It must have been more like five, 'cause I remember hearin' these things when I was goin' for my first sign up for kindergarten school. To this day, I remember these women's names, and I have to try real hard to not be bitter with them. The Lord helps me with it; see, it's all part of the journey.

The neighborhood we lived in had the houses kinda lookin' alike. There were lots o' sycamore trees, dirt roads, muddy dug-out ditches, and I can't remember no mailboxes. Our house and the ones on both sides had yards, but they was real small. Lots of times we was stuck indoors 'cause we'd be real sick. When we was well enough to hang out with neighbor kids, I remember bad things that I don't really want to remember—things that we did with them 'cause they was the closest children 'round. This one family had kids that, well, they was a lot older and seems they had lots o' time on their hands. It was apparently these kids that educated us little ones; they was real comfortable tellin' us all about our and their bodies—makin' it seem kinda matter o' fact. They'd say, "All kids play this game, you know, the one called 'you show me yours . . . I'll show you mine.'" We kinda knew that stuff wasn't right, makin' most o' them memories unpleasant now, and I wish we'd known enough to say, "No, we ain't playin' those games." But we was really at risk bein' just curious children with no one around actin' much like a parent. Our mom at this time was so depressed, she spent more and more time starin' 'round into empty space with her eyeballs all glazed over. There wasn't no one for teachin' us values, no one for teachin' us we should be keepin' these things private. It was like most of the times, we was just raisin' ourselves.

Worse than Death

It was around this time, when I was five, well, I remember a really bad—in fact, it was one of the worst times that I can *ever* remember. Our daddy started actin' more and more abusive with our mama. Seems like he'd just come home and beat her to a pulp, with us children watchin' and feelin' every blow he was givin' our mama. Neglectin' and leavin' us—that's what he did best.

This one winter, I remember our family got real sick. Usually when we got sick, it happened to us as a whole family; this was no 'ception. It was terrible; we was all feelin' just awful 'cause of these worms livin' inside us. They must have been tapeworms 'cause they was 'bout three to four inches long, and everybody in the whole family was infested with them things. We had two big, rusty-tin coal buckets that sat around the stove. With all of us gettin' immediate and sudden cramps and 'bouts of sickness, we couldn't always make it to the outdoor toilet. In emergencies, we'd just use those buckets; and after a time, well, those buckets was alive with them worms. The worst part was that the longer we was sick, we sometimes coughed up worms; we felt them in our nose and mouth, and we passed them indoors when they got real bad. We were all so sick—I think those creatures made us real anemic, tired, and made our stomachs hurt more than anyone can 'magine. It was purty near impossible to sleep 'cause we hurt so bad; didn't help we was starvin' hungry every night, too. I wonder sometimes why we all didn't die. That awful pain in my stomach is still fresh in my memory.

While we was so sick, there was one day, it was probably the single most painful day of my life ever! Two stranger men in fine pressed suits came bangin' on our door. I must have stayed home from school 'cause of the worms, and so there was my mama home with four small children ages 'bout five years and under. Sudden-like, these men was demandin' to come in the door—they forced my poor little mama to just let them in. They told her that they had legal papers and rights to take all her children. My mama was just devastated; she started cryin', beggin', and pleadin'. All us children started screamin'. The men, they just scooped us up and fought our mama off as she clawed at them and begged them to leave us alone. They took us and quick-like started shovin' and stuffin' us in their big shiny car. All the while, my mama kept yellin', swearin', and beggin' them to leave us alone. She was hangin' onto their polyester suits and clawin' at their backs all the while they was shovin' us into that car's huge fake leather-covered seats. I still remember how they felt, how they smelt, and how they stuck to our bare, skinny legs.

Seemed like forever, but they finally got everybody in, so quick, they slammed and locked the doors, and the car started to pull away. It's real clear for me—I was lookin' with my nose pressed up to that passenger window toward my mama. It was hard to see 'cause the dust was blowin' as the tires was spinnin'. All of us were so scared and near hysterical, and we saw our mama just layin' in the dirt road, poundin' the gravel, clawin' down into the dirt for rocks to throw at the car. She kept screamin' as loud as she could. Ignorin' her, the men just kept drivin'. There was Ray and James in the front seat, 'cause they was babies. Then there was Melissa, nicknamed Missy, and me in the back. I was sure, I really *knew*, we just *had* to pay attention, 'cause we had to remember how to get back home.

The fear and the pain was almost more than I could stand.

We had no idea where we was goin' and why this was happenin'. These men did not bother to 'splain anythin' to us. Thank God, now things have changed through the DSS (Department of Social Services), but back then, they didn't have to tell nobody nothin'. Finally, they got frustrated with the babies 'cause they was cryin' so bad; angry-like, these men, they shoved the little ones back to me and Missy, and we clung to our precious babies and we all cried together. Seemed like we drove forever, but after awhile, we pulled up to a nice house. These men, they tore the babies from us and started settlin' and squishin' both them into one guy's arms—I was so 'fraid for my precious brothers, I thought I'd just die. All of a sudden, the pain in my heart was worse than the pain in my stomach. I had this gosh-awful, horrible feelin' that I would never see them again and there weren't nothin' I could do to keep these guys from takin' them. So my brothers got carried into that house, and soon as the welfare guy came back without them, I demanded to know where they were. He told us the babies were just goin' to stay there with a family for a while. I tried to feel better by promisin' myself in my head over and over that somehow I'd get help and we'd be together and we'd have a safe home again. Still, nothin' helped; and that day, it truly was the absolute worst day in my life!

Mountain Mission School

These men, they took me and Missy to a place called Mountain Mission School—a rundown orphanage for kids that wasn't wanted. I didn't think I belonged there 'cause I knew our mama wanted us and we all wanted each other. When Missy and I got there, it was about the same time as our other sisters and brothers were bein' delivered; they'd been picked up from their schools. We were all kinda herded into this big cookin' area, like a huge industrial kitchen. This place didn't have bathtubs with runnin' water; they just had big washtubs. I remember that it kinda felt like we was in processin'; they handled us one at a time. There were two or three mean, hateful women, and they each took turns watchin' over the herd of us children. One would take a child and remove their clothes, and the other woman would scrub the child—sometimes rubbin' so hard it hurt; then they'd start rinsin' us off, grabbin' us and dryin' us real rough. Anything they took off us, they threw in the stove. I understand now that maybe they was tryin' to fight disease and stuff, but these women had no business workin' with orphans—they was angry-like and jerkin' us all around. They just made the whole thing even worse. It was an awful first-day experience we had at this place. We was so afraid, 'cause we knew we was at the mercy of strangers; we was all filled with hurt and paralyzin' fears.

I remember after this intense cleanin', they put some clothes on us and shoved each of us toward "our" room—tellin' us this place was where we'd be stayin'. They put me in a room with a girl who was a teenager, and I was only five years old. Well, this girl was so messed up in the head; I felt sad for whatever made her that way, but she was really emotionally sick. She'd pet my hair and tell me how beautiful I was and how sweet I was; and then, in the same breath, she would slam me up against the wall and tell me how worthless I was. This started immediately when I got in the room; she didn't know me from Adam, for sure, and I couldn't understand how she could be so mean to me, a total stranger and just a little girl. I didn't understand mental illness, but this girl was just not all there—plus she was unpredictable, ugly, mean, and angry. Things just seemed to be going from bad to worse with her 'round.

I remember that our job was to keep the room tidy, and we was supposed to make up our bed. I had never made up a bed before, but that didn't stop me from tryin' hard to be doin' my best. The problem was, I'd be on one side o' the bed, and she'd be on the other. I'd be concentratin' real hard to do foldin' and tuckin' just right. When we'd finish makin' the sheets and covers look real neat, she'd rip all them off, smush them on the floor, stomp on them, hit me, and throw me around. She'd start yellin' and tellin' me how I weren't no good at nothin'. I'd see my other siblin's in the cafeteria area sometimes 'cause we all had breakfast and supper together. Each day, feelin' desperate, I'd always try nonstop to 'splain to my sister Mary what was happenin' to me. I think she did try to talk to some of the teachers or somethin', but they didn't never believe her. So the terror I faced from my unpredictable roommate continued till I finally got to go home.

Anyway, these days at this Mountain Mission School, with all these other unwanted children, were almost all awful. The only good days came on some Sundays when our mama and daddy were allowed to visit. I remember seein' my mama, and, well, she wasn't eatin', so she was just wastin' away. Even before we got taken away, she was just skin and bones and always so tiny, and I remember now she was also lookin' real weak. People had to help her walk, and I kept thinkin' I needed to be there at home so I could take care of her. We was all hangin' onto hope every Sunday—hope that she'd be better, and somehow we'd get to be back with her. It was awful waitin' to get to go home. The *only* good things about stayin' at the orphanage were that I got to ride a tricycle and eat animal crackers— both these things was totally new to me, and I loved them!

It seems like we was inside that orphanage for three to four weeks, and then there was this court date. There wasn't much investigatin' done before the court date. There we was at the appointed time—it was scary, all of us children lined up on what looked like church pews, with a bigger 'n life judge elevated 'bove us sittin' 'hind some huge wood desk thing in front o' him. All we knew was we had to be real quiet. In that courtroom, no one argued when one of my aunts agreed to be our guardian, and we quick got released to go with her. There wasn't much of a decision or promise from her to keep us in her house instead of lettin' us go back home. So, that's exactly what she did—she sent us right back to be with our family.

This meant we had to start movin' a lot to hide from welfare. All a sudden we'd leave real fast from one shack and go on to the next, and 'cause o' that, we never had hardly anything as far as belongings. Personal stuff would've just slowed us down. I was glad that at least we'd usually find livin places in close by areas so the familiar schools made things a little less frightenin'. Still, some of my memories 'bout what we'd been through started floodin' my mind; it'd been so awful that I couldn't never forget it.

Movin was tough, but bein' back with mama and my siblings helped me start some healin'. I was beginnin' to think a new idea, one that I guess God was puttin' in my head. Little by little, this new idea started replacin' the hatin' and blamin' those women—the ones Mama told us had ratted us out, causin' us to be snatched from our family. I remember wonderin': did God cause the welfare to come take us to save our lives? If He had not used drastic measures, wouldn't we've just gotten sicker and sicker? So maybe—no, almost for sure—social services, them takin' us, the worst thing it seemed could have ever happened, was maybe for the best.

Now that I'm older 'n' understandin' His ways more, I can actually praise God, 'cause without them removin' us from our home, we woulda probably died from them worms. Ain't that just like God? I've found so many times in my life that sometimes whatever seems like the worst thing ever for me, it can be *His* best thing for me. Today I'm sure o' one thing: God used forceful measures to get us children safe, and now I can say, "Hallelujah! Amen!" Bein' real honest, though, I can't yet sing praises specific 'bout those welfare men; I'm still workin' on that one!

Like I said, even though we'd be movin' from house to house lots, it felt so good to carry on at the same secure, safe school. I remember lovin' group music lessons at my elementary school—'cept that sometimes we'd be singin' songs or whatever in a big group, and I could see clear everyone comin' into our school. If ever I saw a man with a suit on that I did not recognize as a teacher, a worker, or somebody I knew, I'd go into this frenzy and panic. Mind racin', I'd start thinkin' about tryin' to develop an escape plan—some way to try to get where I could hide so they couldn't take me back to that orphanage place. My whole body, it would actually tremble all over. The other kids would ask what was wrong, but I didn't dare tell them. That same panic happened most all my growin'-up years—it took a long while for me to finally realize that not everybody that had a suit on worked for the welfare.

One Rescued

You can 'magine how bad it was bein' in that orphanage and then havin' to move 'round so much—it just made me panicked at times. But I did have one sister I could count on—one I wanted to be just like, one who's always tried to live for the Lord. Even at a very young age, she was always willin' to give me support. She was steady, kind, and sure of herself. I believe that had somethin' to do with the fact that she was rescued from our family for a while when she was in 'bout the fifth grade and I was only 'bout a year old.

Uncle Charlie, Daddy's brother, was at a family gatherin' with us, and he was 'splainin about the fact that he and his wife couldn't have no children. Since Daddy had so many kids, Uncle Charlie went and said, "You have so many children, maybe, just maybe, would you give us just one child?" Daddy let him pick one, and he chose my sister Mary. Later on, when we was grown, Uncle Charlie told us he picked the most needy one. Mary was kinda withdrawn cause she was tongue-tied bein' that her tongue was twisted and attached completely to the inside bottom of her mouth makin' it impossible for her to talk right. Plus, she had extremely crossed eyes—she musta been a pitiful sight. Even though I think she's highly intelligent, she probably came across as mentally handicapped back then—so he picked the one who needed him the most. She was with Uncle Charlie one and a half years. During this time, she got surgery to fix her eyes and release and restore her tongue to normal.

I know none of this help woulda been happenin' if Mary had stayed in our family.

After Mary'd been away awhile, Daddy started realizin' that one of his children was really happy, so he was kinda jealous. I'm not sure he knew it, but he really messed up things for Mary by goin' and demandin' to have her back. She said that time away was the best time of her childhood. She had everything a child desires: attention, support, food, clothing, and adults who loved her and loved each other. To be ripped from them and brought back to us was so sad. It seemed that Daddy wanted Mary back 'cause he thought she had value now that someone else wanted her. She became Daddy's favorite from that point on.

In fact, when Uncle Charlie and Aunt Sue'd come to visit, they'd dote on Mary the whole time. I'd be thinkin', *Wait a minute; I'm here too!* They treated her like she was made of gold; they just couldn't keep their hands off her. Mama started gettin' more and more jealous 'cause Daddy and his relatives liked Mary so much. One day, with us all knowin' Mama couldn't stand Aunt Sue, out of the blue, our mama stopped using Mary's real name; instead, she called Mary "Sue" real sarcastic-like. This went on forever. It hurt Mary real bad, but she still enjoyed bein' Daddy's favorite.

What's so amazin' to me is that Mary come back from Uncle Charlie's with value, courage, and self-worth that stayed with her; some of the rest of us never had a chance to feel such things. She was different, makin' me always look up to her and wantin' to be like her. In fact, bein' like Mary became my dream. She moved out when she was fifteen and found another family to live with, followin' the pattern of all us kids. But even from a distance, Mary's remained an amazin' Christian role model for me, someone I loved and respected. She was wise and always knowin' right from wrong. She knew and lived God's word and stood up for it. I saw her walk through many valleys as we was growin' up, but she's stayed steadfast in the Lord. She was and still is quick to say her faith in God is what carried her through each trouble; He alone gave and continues to give her hope. A blessin', that's what Mary was and is to me. I'm grateful for how Uncle Charlie helped her and how that allowed her always bein' there for me.

Kindergarten Through First Grade

As strong as Mary was, one sibling wasn't enough to erase all my fears and insecurities. Bein' at the orphanage made for me some long-lastin' terrifyin' times. Before kindergarten and first grade, me and my mama had never been anywhere away from each other, and I never went anywhere without her. So beginnin' school, I had separation anxiety to the extreme. I musta cried every day. My mama and the other kids, they had to drag me to the bus, and two of the biggest girls in school had to sit on me once I got on that bus. I thought if only I could wiggle out and get to the door, I could start runnin' and find my way home. It ain't no wonder that I can still remember those girls' names—Pat and Beverly; I was so angry at them. And I remember my sweet teacher, who tried everythin' to make me happy, but I cried lots most every day of kindergarten.

I kept it to myself, but in kindergarten, I remember having my first crush. I don't know why that was, and I've always asked myself, "Does everybody have their first crush in kindergarten?" There was this little boy, Joey Yates. He had purty blond hair, and he also had a lot of quarters—not sure which one I liked best 'bout him. I knew you could buy ice cream with quarters. At our school, we always had a snack break every day for the kids if they brought their money. Of course, I didn't have no money. Break time would have been awful for me 'cept for Mrs. Yates, my kindergarten teacher. She wasn't related to Joey, but she was wonderful! She bought my ice cream every single day. The taste of that sweet vanilla ice cream slidin' down my throat—I'll never forget that. I don't know how she did it. I found out later that she had kindness for more than just me. Turns out all us kids, includin' the ones behind and 'fore me in school, well, we all had our snacks bought by Mrs. Yates.

So, I want to salute Mrs. Yates for all the ice cream and for other nice things she did. In her class, I remember I had a problem a lot: when I went to sleep, my bladder would relax. I don't know why and I don't know what kind of condition it could have been, but I wet the bed until I was in the fifth grade. So you can imagine that I didn't want to take no naps at school. When I did fall asleep, Mrs. Yates always had a spare pair of pants for me. Strangely enough, the other kids, they didn't notice I was wearin' different pants after nap time. It was kinda our secret routine: anytime I needed it, she always took those smelly, wet pants and panties home and brought me back washed, clean ones the next day. Thank you, Mrs. Yates!

In the first grade, I had a wonderful teacher, Mrs. Vyres. She opened up the world to me and taught me to read. Kind and patient—that was Mrs. Vyres. She'd make it a point to be lookin' at me, 'specially at my eyes, and she'd say, "Karen, your eyebrows grow together." Then she'd ask me if I knew what that meant. Every time I always said, "No! What?" She was real quick to tell me, "That means you're gonna be rich someday when you grow up." You know what? Her just lookin' into my eyes and talkin' to me made me feel special. I used to wish I was her little girl. I have always remembered this tiny little bit of encouragement, and, well, I believed the story 'bout the eyebrows until I got real big. You know somethin' else? I just knew I could stand whatever came my way, 'cause I knew I was gonna be rich someday.

It was about this time that I was hospitalized with measles. I don't know why I missed my vaccination, but I know that I was really, really sick with all those red spots and feelin' so hot I thought I'd catch fire. Plus, it was lonely 'cause I musta been the first one of us kids to get measles-sick. I was in the hospital all by myself, and thank goodness, this is the only time I ever remember being stuck anyplace all alone.

The only good news from this time was that every body was so good to me, the nurses and all. I remember gettin' lots of ice cream, popsicles, and ginger ale, which was nice. Still, I'd cry every day 'cause I missed my mama. She stayed with me a little, but those times when I was all alone, I was really scared. When they was comin' to pick me up 'cause I was leavin' out of the hospital, four or five more of my brothers and sisters were gettin' dropped off and admitted with the same fever 'n' spots—they all had me to thank for the measles. It was lonely at home then; I was left wanderin' around by myself till they got well.

Summertime: Rosy's Comin'!

The day Mama was 'bout to have baby twelve, my sister Rose Maggeline (Mama was tryin' to get a name from the Bible, but she didn't get the spellin' right; we quick decided to call her Rosy, anyway), Mama musta known she was gonna deliver. See, that mornin' she told my daddy, "I think I'm goin' be deliverin' real soon," but he kinda ignored her and took off to visit some drinkin' buddies. Mama started havin' those pains and gettin' worried, so she sent us kids after Daddy, one after the other 'fore anyone could even get shoes on. Runnin' in bare feet down the dirt road, we was so scared for Mama, each one tryin' to run fastest, be first to find and tell Daddy he gotta go home and get Mama with the truck real quick.

We each seen him sittin' on the porch havin' fun drinkin' and tellin' stories; he just kept sittin' till enough us kids was sent to make him notice. Actin' mad and bothered, he shoved all us messenger kids in the back of the truck, complainin' he weren't ready to leave but he was knowin' he'd never hear the end o' things till he did. We got home, and Mama was real bad hurtin' and all hunched over, so the older kids, they had to carry her to the truck. My daddy never carried my mama anywheres; he was always just concerned 'bout hisself. I remember thinkin' as us kids got her set in that big safe truck seat, "This is one time havin' a nice truck's helpin' out more than just Daddy."

Roy and me, we plain refused to get out. Daddy was runnin' 'round each side of the truck, grabbin' at us, but we was dodgin' and real determined! Roy was the leader of family defiance, so I just went along; if Roy was goin', I was goin' too. If he was gettin' by with it, I could too. So with his support, there was no way 'round it. I *was* goin' with my mama, 'cause it felt like she was gonna have that baby in that truck 'fore we'd get anywheres close to the hospital.

The big kids was supposed to stay home keepin' the little ones, and Daddy argued with me for 'bout five minutes (musta seemed like a year to Mama)—he was determined I couldn't go. "Please, we gotta go and go right *now!*" Mama was beggin' at Daddy. Guess he knew I wasn't gonna budge, so he finally just drove on, fast as he could, to the hospital.

I ain't never before or never since heard screamin' like on that drive. Mama'd be yellin', then stoppin' to breathe, then startin' to yell again, and 'course I could hear everythin' 'cause Daddy he wouldn't use AC for us family—it was "winders down" for us. Bein' so 'fraid for her, I smushed my face to that truck cab window and watched Mama the whole time. At one point, I saw her, rigid arms and palms down, pressin' on the seat to keep her body from sittin' down all the way. Bein' so weak 'n' in pain, she was strugglin' really bad. Stubborn as ever, Daddy parked in the hospital parkin' lot purty far away from the E R.

"I *can't* walk, I *can't* sit—you gotta get me to that door," she screamed.

Some hospital person seein' and hearin' all this brung a wheelchair real fast.

I was probably 'bout seven years old and had no idea where babies come from, so the wheels in my mind started turnin' with big questions: "What's walkin' and sittin' got to do with havin' a baby?" All my wonderin' stopped 'cause o' Mama and Daddy arguing.

In the midst of it all, sensin' she couldn't win no fight with Daddy, Mama finally hollered out real angry and desperate, "If I get outa this truck 'n' sit in that chair, it'll break my baby's neck."

Hearin' those words, that hospital guy started runnin'; I was so glad seein' him comin' back with a stretcher. Talk 'bout frightened—I couldn't barely breathe seein' them wheelin' Mama off! I'm sure Rosie's head was already deliverin' in that truck, so Mama just finished pushin' and deliverin' her baby while they rolled her inside. She lost so much blood that day. I remember hearin' the doctors sayin' they weren't gonna release her till Daddy checked in to have a vasectomy. See, Mama was too weak to have her tubes tied, and she near died birthin' Rosie; the doctors said, havin' one more child would almost certain kill her.

Second Grade

In second grade, I had a teacher named Mrs. Hutchinson, and she was so nice. She looked like an angel, and I loved her. She even smelled beautiful. It was in her class and at this age that teachers were havin' to teach us about brushin' our teeth. Mrs. Hutchinson was determined to impress us about dental hygiene. She had these red tablets you could chew up and they would show her all the stuff on our teeth. I didn't even have a toothbrush, so, of course, I'd lie. I figured, why not fib, sayin' I brushed my teeth every day 'cause I couldn't wait to get one of those big stars beside my name. I'm sure Mrs. Hutchinson knew 'bout my lyin', but still, she wanted real bad for me to come spend Christmas with her that year. I musta been just pitiful 'cause she talked with my siblin's and family for almost a month tryin' to persuade them to let me come stay with her. She just wouldn't give up askin'. But I think my family was afraid she might keep me and not bring me back or somethin', so they wouldn't let me go. I spent my days starin' at her and wishin' with all my second-grade heart she'd take me home with her.

During this year, it was the first time I realized that if you are poor, sometimes you get falsely accused of bad things just 'cause you don't have much. Mrs. Hutchinson, well, she was out sick, and the sub teacher had put her purse on the shelf that was behind the wall next to her desk. Well, anyway, she got missin' somethin' out of her purse, and she was quick and strong in thinkin' that I took it. In fact, I remember her questionin' me over and over and over in front of the whole class. Gosh, I cried that whole day 'cause I kept feelin' like she was thinkin' I took her belongin's. Then it started me thinkin' that she must think I needed it worse than anyone else, and that's why she musta thought surely I was the one who stole from her. It hurt me so bad, and I felt just awful. The other kids in the class decided I was probably the guilty one, too, and they treated me real bad after that day.

Also about this time, I remember we was gettin' ready for the big Christmas party at school, and I was already mad 'cause my family wouldn't let me go spend Christmas with Mrs. Hutchinson's family. I really wanted to go 'cause I just knew I coulda seen what Christmas was really like. At our home durin this time we was eatin' whatever my mama could uncover under the snow, and it was usually this weed we called "mouse-ear." Bein' a vine that grows all year long, we'd still find it in the winter when everything else was gone. We didn't have no salt to go on it or bread to go with it, so we just ate it like it was—a boiled weed. I would sure have loved to be with Mrs. Hutchinson and maybe have somethin' better—I'd never had turkey, dressing, cranberries, pumpkin pie, much less a yeast risin' roll with real butter on it!

I was gettin' more excited every day as my class was plannin' for the Christmas party comin' up; we was gonna have cupcakes, chips, candy, and wonderful things. I'd dream, mouth waterin', about all the goodies; I knew they'd be lots better comparin' to the cooked weeds we was eatin' at home. So I couldn't hardly wait. But on the very day of all the fun and food, I woke up and started throwin' up everywhere; I was so sick. My family looked at my skin and said they just knew I had chicken pox! They said I was gonna have to stay home, but I was determined, even as a second grader. I'd made up my mind, and I *was* goin' to school! You gotta remember, school meant school lunch and school snacks! I was determined to somehow win out and make my way there.

It didn't take long for me to come up with a plan: when the other kids went out the door I'd run out with them and, quick I'd get to the front of the pack and dash way ahead of them all. It worked! I was real fast on my feet and kept a good distance between me, my mom and the other siblings. They all chased me for a while but each one gave up and started walkin as they watched me run out of sight. Since they was only walkin, I had time to circle back, hide and wait for the right moment. Seein' my chance, I come up right behind them as they was gettin on the bus. Pushin my way up the bus steps I could hear mama's voice fadin as she kept yellin, "you get back here, Karen, you here!" I knew my siblings would leave me alone cause I was purty strong and could fiercely hold onto my bus seat; plus none of them had chickenpox yet and didn't want to get too close. So I was pretty happy and proud when I made it all the way to my school and my classroom.

Sittin' in my class anxiously waitin' for the roll call to be over, I was eager to be safe and counted present; then, I'd get to stay if no one noticed the spots. My hopes got interrupted when I saw my sister Theresa; she appeared at my teacher's desk, and shortly after that, Mrs. Hutchinson quietly and sadly called me up. I could tell her heart was breakin' for me. She lifted up my shirt and saw the chicken pox. She said, "Karen, I'm so sorry, but you really have to go home." Callin' the janitor of the school meant he'd be takin' me to the mouth of the holler and be leavin' me for the scary, lonely walk home. I knew my sister Theresa had ratted on me, and I set it in my heart that I was gonna get her back somehow! I went home and had to eat more mouse-ear that day; it was green when I ate it and red when I threw it up—meanin', lookin' back, I guess I was throwin' up blood.

Everybody Knew

In third grade, I had a teacher named Mrs. Fletcher, and she was real sweet but she didn't acknowledge me very much. As the days went on, I was really beginnin' to start figurin' out the differences between me and everybody else, and one was that I wasn't shy. Also, I may not have known much book stuff, but there was another thing I was learnin' for certain at this time: *I was the poorest, ugliest, and dirtiest kid in school. And as if that weren't bad enough, what made it worse was that I started realizin' that everybody knew I was the worst-off kid around.* I remember that everybody at Christmastimes and birthdays would talk about all the gifts, presents, goodies, foods, and parties they'd got. I started feelin' so tired of hearin' about how many and what kind of presents and fun times everybody else was gettin', so I just started to make up stuff that I got, lyin' as creative as I could. Of course, nobody believed me. Still, I'd just 'magine up pictures about stuff that I wished I'd got. I'd tell other kids all about wild and fancy things I'd got at surprise parties and the like. I figured, "what the heck"; it didn't make much difference to my life.

God?

Thinkin' about God probably happened when I was in third grade and about seven or eight. I remember I used to pray 'cause my gramma had taught me a little bit about the person in heaven. All I knew was that there was some great being somewhere and *He* was in charge and I could ask *Him* for things. So, I would just keep askin' and askin', even though it didn't appear to me that anybody was listenin'.

About this time in my life, I really started hatin' seein' my daddy come home. In fact, all us kids, we all kinda hated the weekends 'cause he'd come home after gettin' paid and he'd bring extra drunks and plenty of liquor and beer along with him. One in particular was his brother, my uncle. Everybody called him "Red" 'cause he died his hair red; in our eyes he was a nasty pervert, and that's the truth. They would drink and it would always end in the same scene: they'd be yellin' at my mama 'cause she couldn't serve them good enough as far as food or whatever they wanted. And even if she did give them stuff they liked, my daddy would start pickin' at the way she looked. His favorite put-down was to tell 'bout her breast lookin' like fried eggs. See, she was so skinny from lack o' food. We got to eat at school, but Mama didn't have nothin'. After tearin' down how she looked, he'd start jokin' how bad she cooked. Truth is, she didn't have no supplies and no one to teach her 'bout recipes 'n' such. So, seemed like Daddy was havin' fun abusin' her or terrorizin' the whole family. It got ordinary that 'bout Thursday, we'd all start dreadin' the weekend; come Friday, we'd be feelin' awful as we seen him arrivin' home.

I remember one particular evenin', he was late comin' home; Mama put everybody in the bed (we slept all together)—there was six in one bed. We was kinda like a litter of puppies, and we loved cuddlin' up together. I remember gettin' on my knees after everybody else went to sleep, and I said, "Please, God—just kill him on the way here." I asked God to do whatever He had to do to just stop him so he couldn't come home no more. Well, the next mornin', I got up and things seemed real quiet. I was lookin' around and went into my mama's room. I saw someone in her bed, and his whole head was bandaged—like totally covered with white gauze that had spots of blood seepin' through. Of course, it was Daddy and he was drunk and passed out, so I went to see my mama and asked her what had happened. She said Daddy had got drunk and drove his truck off into the Lavista River, and that he 'bout died.

So, as a child I kept wonderin' to myself: *Could this happen 'cause I prayed?* I took responsibility for what I'd asked God for. I felt horrible and walked around feelin' the weight of the world 'cause I thought I had wished that wreck onto my daddy. Now I know better, and I understand that God has His way, *His* will, no matter whatever I'd say or ask for, and *His* will is what gets done. Still, as a child, I remember how bad I felt and how I knew I might have cost the whole family its transportation and the only daddy we knew. I felt really bad.

Fear at Home, Safety at School

When I was in the fourth grade, we lived in an old, abandoned, two-story house at the head of Stiltner's Creek. When we moved in, somebody let my daddy down into the well with a rope so he could clean out the dead rats that was floatin' 'round in the water. 'Cept for the rats, the well was really nice 'cause it had a crank thing so we could wind up the rope and pull up the bucket when it was full. That was a whole lot better than havin' to pull up all them buckets by hand.

To get to school, we would walk about a mile to catch a truck that took us out to the mouth of the holler to catch the bus. The school system paid a woman to use her truck in the holler 'cause everyone knew a bus couldn't never have made it on the bad road. I still remember the truck driver, Priscilla Fields; she took me home to spend the night with her and gave me a bath once. Why was she so kind to me? Now, I know it must have been God. So, the truck picked us up and brought us to the designated spot about a mile from home every mornin' and dropped us off in the afternoon. Lookin' back, it's kinda scary that nobody could get a vehicle closer to our house than that. Bottom line, it's safe to say we did a whole lot o' walkin'.

At this time in my life, well, I guess I was learnin' to tell time, and I remember startin' to watch the clock. It was the fourth grade, and I had a teacher named Mr. Vanover. He was kinda short, and I thought he was terribly handsome. In springtime, I'd pick him flowers as I walked the holler toward the truck. I remember after 'bout the first month of school every day as school ended, I'd start worryin'. I kinda felt let down 'cause we'd be leavin' all the fun and safety I felt with Mr. Vanover. I truly didn't want to go home 'cause I felt really secure at school and around this teacher. He was so steady, and he had no scary surprises—that's why I liked him so much. He never got mad or tried to embarrass me when I couldn't remember my times tables. Anytime I got the chance, I'd give him flowers I'd done picked, and I started waitin' for the day that he would proclaim to the world that I would be his wife. Never mind that he was a newlywed that year.

The part of the holler we walked on, well, there were mines—little caves dug out on the side of the road and in the side of the mountain. They was big dark holes that looked like homes for bears, mountain lions, or all sorts of scary stuff just waitin' to gobble me up. My sisters and I would always walk home together, and sometimes as we'd be gettin' close to one of these mines, I'd see them look at each other. They'd always give each other "the eye," and the fear would quick grip my heart. You see, after that signal, they'd take off runnin' as fast as they could, and there I'd be, left near one of them caves by myself. I was such a chicken and I was so scared of somethin' terrible that might be livin' in there. Plus, to make matters worse, I'd have to go pee, and everybody would just go ahead—no one would stop for me. So, naturally I'd usually wet my pants. There I'd be with wet pants, fallin' down and cryin', and they would keep runnin' as hard and fast as they could. They'd be laughin' and gigglin' 'cause of the way I would bolt after them, screamin' and howlin' like somethin' already had got hold o' me. They was only kids, too, and really they didn't have no idea how all this was affectin' me.

Alone with My Problems

I had so much wrong with me and my life—if it wasn't my ears, it was my kidneys, or it was really bad weather in that lonely holler; sometimes it sure wasn't fun. The only time it wasn't too bad was if I didn't fall or have to go pee and if it didn't rain. Most days we had to roll up our britches' legs and take our shoes off to cross big creeks. It wasn't so bad in the summer, but in the winter, the water was like ice. Sometimes the mud would be so deep we kept our shoes off, tyin' them together and hangin' them 'round our neck. When I didn't have no shoelaces, it was a real problem. At the truck pickup place, we'd be tired, wet, and muddy, but still havin' to put back on our shoes. All in all, walkin' in that holler was a pain.

Like I mentioned, I had troubles with my ears; guess they was really bad infections, one right after the other. We didn't know nothin' 'bout middle ear problems, so my family, they was always comin' up with home remedies that made no sense. Somebody told Mama to pour hot pee fresh from my body into my ears. When that didn't work, they told her to have someone blow warm cigarette smoke in my ear. Neither one of these treatments ever helped, but at least they was tryin'. So, truth is, nothin' fixed my problem, and my ears hurt all the time. We didn't know back then to associate it with me bein' real clumsy. Sometimes as a joke, people would call me "Grace." I'd be fallin' all the time on the way to school and I'd get covered with mud. My sisters would act kinda disgusted and make me go all the way back home up that awful holler by myself. I was so scared and panic-feelin'. See, we knew there was panthers in that holler 'cause one got after my brother and he barely got away and we saw the scary footprints. So, I'd run as fast as I could callin' for Mama as loud as I could, always hopin' she would be outside to hear me. Sometimes she'd be there; sometimes she wouldn't. This is how lots of my days went.

I peed in the bed the whole time I was little until about the fifth grade. My mama used to rub my face in it to discourage the accidents, but nothin' would help. I found out when I grew up that my kidneys weren't shaped right and that they were smaller than normal. Of course, I sure didn't know any of this then; all I knew was that I felt there was nothin' I could do on my own to stop the problem. If I went to sleep, my bladder relaxed and that's what would happen. The sad thing is that I slept with a whole bunch of my siblin's, so let's just say I wasn't the favorite of anybody 'cause I peed on everybody.

I think it's funny now, but back then, sometimes kids and teachers kinda avoided me 'cause, to make matters worse, I musta smelled real bad. See, us kids, we'd just wear the same clothes over and over as much as possible. We didn't have pajamas. So I'd pee in the bed in my clothes at night, get up in the mornin', and stand by a coal-burnin' heater. That heater got really, really hot. I'd be so cold and wet that I'd stand as close to it as I could without gettin' burned. After a short stand, big puffs of steam and coal smoke would roll off my clothes, and they'd dry out while I was wearin' them. I thought this was really kinda smart 'cause I could just keep a goin'. I just didn't know that I stunk real bad and that was maybe why kids didn't get too close. Lookin' back, truth was, not only did I stink, but also I figger I must've made my siblin's smell that way too.

She Was Beautiful–She Was Mine

One thing I remember about the fifth grade is that I had big plans to take my favorite doll to show everyone in my new class. My gramma gave me the doll back in the fourth grade, but I waited to take it to school till the next year. That doll, it was kinda my baby 'cause it was totally mine and given just to me, and that's what made it so special. Turns out the dime-store baby doll had belonged to Gramma's daughter—Gramma was old and this was the doll that had belonged to the oldest of her twelve children, meanin' that, of course, the doll had seen its better days. Although her face had somehow stayed purty clean, the rest of her was marked in pencils, pens, and markers on every inch of her vinyl-covered body, 'cept for her fingers and toes, which done been chewed off. Even worse was that her hair looked like it'd been burned off. But still *I loved her*, and *she was mine*. I put love and carin' into her, makin' her some clothes out of old rags bein' saved for gnat fires.

I remember exactly the day when I took her to school; I felt so protective and proud of that baby doll. But purty quick, it made me really sad 'cause people was laughin' at that pathetic doll and makin' fun of it and of me. I hanged onto my relationship with that doll. I kinda felt related to her, and I never stopped lovin' her or thinkin' she was beautiful! I took her back home, and I never brought her to school again. I was determined to protect her from any more abuse.

How Bein' Poor Feels

This whole time as I was growin' up, my daddy was so mean to us, but he would mostly be mean to my mama. He would come home from work on payday and have wads of money in his pockets, and she'd beg him for a few dollars for groceries. He wouldn't give any of it to her; he'd just ignore her and sit in front of us with his money and his liquor. We knew that sometimes he'd stop off on the way home at some whore's house and give her most of his money; he'd always be very generous with everybody else, but not with us. No wonder we were the beggars in the neighborhood. We had to ask others for everything. And to make matters worse, my daddy, he always had nice trucks—I mean like brand-new ones. So the neighbors, they didn't understand why they should help us when our daddy's drivin' up and down the road in a shiny, big, no-dents truck.

You see, my daddy, well, he most of the time worked in the coal mines, and he'd work two shifts. He was really a hardworkin' man, but he wasn't workin' for his kids—he just didn't care 'bout us. We had so little, and some days I dreaded gettin' home from school. See, most days me and my sister Theresa, we'd walk in and Mama would immediately give us a cup—like a coffee cup. She'd put it in our hands and say, "Go and ask the neighbors for a cup o' meal or cup o' flour or anythin' they can spare." Mama picked Theresa and me cause we was the oldest left at home. See, soon as a sibling got old enough they'd leave to live with other families. So we'd begin our trek around the neighborhood, which was a long ways 'cause people didn't live close to each other in those hills. We'd knock on the doors and stick out the cup and ask for a cup o' whatever they could give; most of the time, they'd say, "No, we don't have it," and slam the door 'cause they got sick of it. Really, I can understand why—they just didn't see why they should help us when our daddy had a nicer vehicle than they had. Sometimes we'd be surprised 'cause they'd give us somethin', but most times, they didn't. I hated beggin' more than anything. Honestly, what made it extra bad was that when me and Theresa came home with an empty cup—well, we just felt like we let the whole family down. I still see my mama and younger siblin's waitin' anxiously; it was so painful showin' them the empty cup.

Two Gifts, Three Girls

Another memory from the fifth grade comes 'round Christmastime. My oldest sister was married, and she had talked my daddy into buyin' us Christmas presents. We'd never had presents before. So Daddy, I reckon, went with my sister; and she, sure thing, told him what to get. Seems he bought each of the three girls, me and Missy and Theresa, a "baby alive." Those were little dolls that ran off batteries, and, of course, he bought the boys somethin' else, but

I sure can't remember what. Anyway, this baby alive was what every girl in the world wanted at that time 'cause it could move its mouth and arms, eat, pee, and stuff. We had no idea we was gonna get anything, especially not this great baby doll. We figgered it'd be just like every other year, and we'd barely have anything to eat and for sure we wouldn't get no presents. So suddenly when Daddy came truckin' home with two of these dolls—this was a Christmastime to remember! He kind o' just threw them at us. They wasn't wrapped or nothin', and it wasn't even quite Christmas yet. He 'splained that we'd have to share. We started figurin' out one of us would be sharin' a doll with another sister 'cause there were three little girls and only two dolls. That was okay, though—we didn't mind. We was so excited. We loved our new babies.

When I went to school after the holidays, there was this girl (I won't mention her name) who lived down the road from us. I remember she had a baby alive with her at school, and she said, "Look what your daddy gave me." I couldn't believe it! I remember my sister Loni bein' upset when she found out that we didn't each get a present and we was all just figurin' out why. This other girl told me, "Your daddy stopped off and gave me this for Christmas." She was always tellin' me about the money Daddy gave her mama, and she always had a list of lots of stuff that he'd bought for her. I didn't know how to handle it. In fact, for a while, I hated this girl, and I did everything I could against her. Now, I have to say, "I'm sorry (to that girl)—I didn't know, it wasn't your fault." Now I understand that my daddy gave stuff to any woman he thought he had a chance with. All his life, he continued to give things to anybody 'cept us. If only someone had confronted my daddy about how bad he treated his family—maybe it mighta helped.

A Million Bucks

In fifth grade, I was dirty, ugly, poor, and I stank, but I was not shy; I don't know why, but I wasn't. Every year at Harmon Elementary, they had a talent show. I loved to sing, and I wanted to be in that show so bad. There were classmates entered who had so many talents, from piano, violin, dancin', singin', and the like. In the midst of all the talent, here comes me. The music teacher volunteered to play me a song, and since I knew "Jeremiah Was a Bullfrog," that was my choice. I remember practicin' in the cafeteria, where the stage and piano sat. It was amazin' 'cause all the lunchroom workers came out to listen. They were each one so kind to me. They'd always be givin' me extra food, and now they were listenin' and clappin' and cheerin' me on. I felt like they thought I was Dolly Parton. I felt like a million bucks! The day of the actual show, my art teacher took me into the bathroom, washed my hair, and gave me some new clothes to wear. So, I got to sing in front of the whole school. I wasn't shy—not sure why, but I wasn't. Guess you know I didn't win, but I had so much fun tryin'.

Talk About Messed-Up

"It would only take just a quick pull and she'd be gone," Daddy would say standing casual-like in the livin' room while holdin' a knife up to Mama's throat. When we lived up in the holler near Stiltner's Creek, this kinda behavior was becomin' almost a common thing for my daddy. All us children would stand around screamin' and cryin'—most of us, we'd be shakin', we was so scared. That was how Daddy got his entertainment, I guess. I tried to hide the knives all the time, but somehow he'd always find them.

One evening in particular, I remember the snow was deep, and in the mountains of Virginia it got really cold; it was totally freezin' that day. We was all gettin' ready for bed when he started sayin' he was gonna shoot "somethin' or someone." He was gettin' so drunk he'd say "pearl" instead of "squirrel" while he was cleanin' his gun. So that night, I just knew he was gonna do somethin' really bad. He sat there with his gun, slobberin' and fallin' all over, and he decided he would start goin' after my mama. Suddenly he ran her around the house a little bit, chasin' her and threatenin' to shoot. And then before we knew it, he ran her right out the door; then he locked her outside, and he wouldn't let her open the door to come back in. So our mama was outside in the snow with no shoes or warm clothes on. My daddy was so mean. We knew Mama was hurtin' from the severe cold, so we hurt, too. We begged him to let us open the door, but he refused and stood guard over it.

That night Mama walked out of the holler with no shoes on her feet. I remember that somebody, a nice person, took her in and called the police to report the problem. The police came, and they drug our daddy out of the house that night. I remember that I was so afraid. Yes, I thought Daddy needed the beatin' he got with the billy stick 'cause he was refusin' arrest, but I was so afraid we wouldn't have anyone if he got taken. So, after a while, my mama, she went back to the jail the next day and dropped the charges. Turns out, there was always somebody gettin' Daddy out o' trouble. The people Daddy worked with, well, they bailed him out lots 'cause they needed him to do his work. Like I said before, there really weren't nobody makin' him learn to do right.

My Mama

I want to take time to talk about my mom. She was born March 13, 1937, in the hills of Virginia. She was the youngest, the thirteenth child, of a sawmiller and his wife in Wolf Pin Holler. Her mother was a busy, hardworkin' woman who made all the family's clothes and soap—all the while tendin' a large garden. Most of Mom's daily care as a new baby named Pearl came from my Aunt Dot, Mom's older sister. By any standard, Pearl was loved and cherished by the entire family, as is often the case concernin' the baby of the family.

She told me her father carried her to the table for breakfast every day and was still doing so when she was eight years old. That's when he was killed in an accident at work. Life for my mama was a lot harder after that, but she had a strong spirit and was always able to be thankful for what she had. Mom didn't go to school 'til she was twelve years old, but she was real proud she graduated sixth grade. She was the only one in her family who could read and write, so she was a big help to all the family around her.

Mama met my daddy at church when she was eighteen, and after a short, well-chaperoned courtship, they were married. They set up housekeeping in a one-room shack—it was horrible, but she would always smile and talk fondly of that time in her life. Not long after the wedding, my daddy became an abusive drunk, and the moonshine and bluegrass music both flowed freely for him. I guess in the area where we lived, it was accepted for the daddy to be a mean-spirited and selfish drunk.

I don't know how my mama stood it. She had five children, and then a set of twin girls, me and my sister Sharon (the one who drowned when she was just two years old). That was when Mama just wanted to die. She was acceptin' all the blame for my sister's dyin'. No one in her life had trainin' to help Mama cope with the grief and guilt, and I'm sure she got more depressed each day.

She kept carin' for all her born and growin' children while she was also havin' more. All this time, she'd be livin' without the things a woman needs: health care, nutrition, love of her husband, and support of friends and family. My mama didn't have the luxury of any close friends, and this breaks my heart, for I never would have made it this far if God had not given me true, godly friends to help me along the way.

I know Mama musta felt isolated 'cause we lived way back in the holler and she didn't have no driver's license or vehicle to go anywhere. So, we almost never went visitin'. It didn't matter much 'cause, truth is, people never really wanted to see such a big crowd as us arrivin' and standin' on their doorstoop anyway.

I remember we lived on a high hill, and my brother and I would stand at the window watchin' my mama try to climb the steep, ice-covered slope to our house. She'd be carryin' a feed sack full o' coal on her back 'cause we needed it to heat the house. She'd take a few steps, fall, catch herself with her bare hands, then get up and fall again. It was hard to watch and hard for her, but she never gave up. She was always doin' stuff for us. Lots o' times, when there was only one piece of bread for all of us to share, she said she wasn't hungry. The love she gave us and the sacrifices she made—well, they made up for our bein' so poor.

Turnin' Point

When my father and my mother forsake me the Lord will take me up. (Ps. 27:40)

It was around this time that I'll never forget—I saw my mama drunk for the first time. Me and some of the other kids was walkin up the holler after school was over and we saw mama sittin' on a log. I said, "What are you doin', Mama?" "I found your daddy's liquor," she said. All times before this when she found his booze, she'd pour it out and then get beaten for it. But this day it changed, and it was the beginnin' of what I'll call "hell." I remember her sayin' over and over,

"If you can't beat 'em, join 'em." So, after that day, we had nobody left 'cause Mama, she had changed. I remember draggin' her up that holler and thinkin', *"Now who do we have? If we're gonna survive, it's up to us.* It was like she just handed me all her responsibilities and the rearin' of my four younger siblin's. I was so angry with life and the loss of my mama. Her body was still around, but it now held a mean, angry, hateful drunk who had to be cared for along with her children. Still, she did the best that she could. I think that day she was just broken, and I knew from then on, she'd be gone from us forever.

And Daddy, well, he stayed just a mean man, and he never thought about us bein' hungry and cold and alone. The house we lived in was so old you could see through the cracks inside the walls all the way to the outdoors. And my mama, well, when she was sober, she fought every day tryin' to keep the house warm. One day she was sawin' wood with this big saw that takes two people, like a bow saw that takes one person on each end. But she only had little children there to help 'cause none of the big kids was home. My brother James got too close and was tryin' to help her hold the log. Well, somehow, the saw caught his finger and almost cut it clear off. Mama tried to bandage it Up, and somehow, by the grace of God, it grew back together. I remember we all felt the pain of the saw that day. It felt like my heart was splittin' 'cause I knew how bad James was hurtin'.

Lots o' times Mama would be tryin' so hard to scrape things together to keep us warm and feed us. She was always lookin' for some stuff that grew wild that we could eat, and she knew where to find it. Also, she'd be lookin' for things to burn, givin' us a way to stay warm. We used to think we'd really hit the jackpot if we could find an old tire or anythin' made of rubber in the woods. The best find was a big truck tire 'cause we could roll them into the fire and it would throw out a lot o' heat. All I remember was bein' so happy 'cause it made me feel warm. We didn't know it was probably toxic, and I ain't sure we woulda cared anyways. It was worth sniffin' dirty smoke if it meant we didn't have to feel so awful cold. Turns out it was surely killin' brain cells. All that thick, black smoke comin' up around us; our faces would be glowin' red-like as we breathed it in. After a short time, it made us all look black standin' round that burnin' tire, but we stayed watchin' till all the rubber melted. We'd be so close to the fire we could even taste the burnt rubber. We didn't care about black faces and hands or what we were inhalin'; we was just so happy to be warm.

Sheer Terror

We lived in one house in Stiltner's Creek that was a two-story house, and, well, I don't think we paid any rent for it or anything. This big house, it had a well in the front yard, which always made me sad remindin' me of my twin sister Sharon and her drownin' when she was only two. Anyway, we figgered it musta been very rich people who lived in this house a long time ago 'cause it seemed like it'd been real nice and gorgeous some time ago. It had a big porch and lots o' rooms, but problem was, when we was there, it was very dilapidated and even kinda frightenin'. To make matters worse, my mama and daddy told us really scary stories about this house and how one of the people who lived there had hung herself in the garden, and another lady who visited the house had killed herself on the back porch.

At bedtime in this house, my mama and daddy started a routine: they would tell us really scary stories before bed most every night. I truly was frightened of my own shadow, so it didn't take much to be puttin' me into a full panic. Plus, of course, we had to go to the outdoor toilet in the pitch-black night, and that kept me bein' so terrified. I was just sure somethin' lurkin' in the dark was gonna grab and carry me off and no one would know it.

One night in particular, my mama started tellin' the ghost stories all on her own. I'm sure my daddy talked her into it, but anyway, the two of them ended by joinin' in together with some horrible endin' to their tale. While we were in bed sound asleep, they decided to put some worn-out, tattered sheets on their heads. Thinkin' they looked real, they began the plannin' to run into our sleepin' room with only the light from the fireplace makin' shadows on their forms. So it started—the walkin' 'round our bed. Since that didn't scare us enough, they grabbed us, shakin' us awake and startlin' us by makin' ghost noises. This new drama, the ghost costumes, and the scary stories they'd tell, well, this made me start hopin' nighttime wouldn't never come.

Although there were lots of nights they tried to scare us, I'll never forget one specific night in particular. I woke up and saw this person in a dirty, stained, torn, white sheet that had ripped out hole openin's for big scary eyes to be starin' at me. This creature's hands was on my shoulders, and they was shakin' me pretty hard. When I totally woke up and realized I wasn't dreamin', I saw these images clear and I got so frightened that I couldn't even breathe—it felt like there was no air! My siblin's said they didn't think I was gonna be able to get my breath back, ever, 'cause I was turnin' blue before I finally gasped for air. Don't know if children can be scared to death, but if so, I surely might have died that night. No matter, Mama and Daddy, they'd do this kind o' thing anyway, lots of nights. Guess it was their fun to see how bad they could scare us.

So, I was always afraid to go to sleep at night. I saved that for the classroom at school.

Hard Times

There was one time and story that is so sad—an animal lover's worst fear—you may not want to read it. I want you to 'magine, if you choose to read it, us children feelin' like the story could just as easily been about us. See, times was real hard up in the head of Stiltner's Creek. We just survived the best we could. One day an old, malnourished dog showed up and just wouldn't leave. She was so desperate to find food, water, and shelter. Guess she kinda knew she needed to provide for the puppies she was carryin'. Once they was born, they grew to be big puppies real quick; there was about six of 'em. The mama was like a German shepherd, and these pups had grown to 'bout two months old. It was gettin' real cold, and we decided to put the mama and pups in a dug-out room under the house so they wouldn't freeze one night. When we went to get them out the next mornin', they was ever one of 'em dead. We was shocked 'cause their feet, ears, tails, and anything else that stuck out was missin'. It was a strange and gruesome sight. Strangely enough, though, there was no blood anywhere—not one drop seen. So we figgered it was what they call wolf rats that killed 'em. These were the only critters that coulda sucked all the blood out of them pups.

I was so sad, and I cried and cried for 'bout a month thinkin' 'bout those puppies and that mama dog. Worse than worryin' for those puppies was that every night as I was goin' to sleep, I kept feelin' frightened, even terrified. See, Mama told us stories 'bout sometimes havin' to knock rats off the bed when they was tryin' to get at us when we was babies. So, some nights, I'd be tryin' to tuck my legs and feet up under my arms and hands, which were holdin' everythin' all up tight-like toward my chest, kinda like doin' a somersault or cannonball. I was so scared that the hungry wolf rats might come back and get some parts o' me. Bein' worried was bad enough, but tryin to maneuver in a bed with six siblins next to me was dang near impossible.

If you're scared of the dentist, you might want to skip the next story. Not too long after them baby dogs was attacked, I remember none of us was sleepin' well. We was all havin' nightmares and wakin' up cryin'. Then, to make matters worse, my mama started havin' an awful time, and we all got so afraid for her. Havin' children one right after the other and poor nutrition is hard on a woman's body. Seems like my mama always had complaints 'bout her bad teeth. So here we were, kinda isolated in Stiltner's Creek, sleep deprived, restless, and Mama got to hurtin' so bad one night with a toothache that she woke us all up swearin'. She said her only relief would be from gettin' her bad tooth out. We didn't even have no aspirin or nothin'. Bein' desperate, she made my sister get ready to pull her tooth with a pair of pliers. It was a back jaw tooth. None of us wanted to hurt my mama, but it seemed like there weren't no other choice; Mama was beggin' for help. It hurt my sister so bad to do this, but somehow while she was shakin' all over and cryin', she managed to hold still enough to grip them pliers 'round that tooth. Then, quick as she could—almost not lookin', she pulled the tooth out, roots and all. It hurt us all pretty bad, 'cause we had to witness the whole excruciating ordeal. When our mama hurt, we hurt, and this was a real bad one. I still cry for my mama and my sister when I look back.

A Lighter Note

I do remember some times when we had fun growin' up near Stiltner's Creek. There was this one time somebody sold—or, no—it was that they gave us two pigs. Only good thing 'bout them pigs was that my brother Roy could ride them for fun. You know what? Most of the time, us kids didn't have no food, but I remember my daddy made sure them dang pigs had food. Some of the times with nothin' for us to eat anywheres in the house, my mama would mix water with pig food and bake it, feed it to us, and we'd eat it! It kept our stomachs from gnawin' on our backbones. I remember the food was called Midlands pig food, and it was supposed to be mixed up like slop for your hogs. But, uh, I hate to think what was in that animal feed. I don't think I'll ever bring myself to look at the ingredients on a package of that stuff—I mean never! But I know it kept our bellies from hurtin' so bad, so we ate it—and it didn't kill us. So, I guess we was okay. I guess—no, I know—I can thank God for pig food.

Anyway, I remember livin' up there in that holler and that there were actually some good times. We played outside a lot. We could run around with no shirts on 'cause we lived so far from anybody. I remember somebody took a picture of me, probably 'cause it looked funny with no shirt while I was seemin' so proud that I had a pocketbook over my shoulder. I think it was in the third grade or sometime around that age. That picture—me with only hand-me-down pedal pushers on—standin' proud with a thrift-store pocketbook strung over my bare shoulder, smilin' like a mule eating briers. Well, it showed things as they was.

Who Don't Like Fairs, Parades, and Sleepovers?

I now have children of my own, two grown children and I also have a four-year-old, and I have decided that I just hate fairs and I just hate parades and some other fun things. I never knew why, and I used to feel so guilty for not likin' these things—but now I know, well, at least I think I know, the reason I despise these things. It's because they are linked back to my childhood. My daddy, uh, he didn't take us anywhere much. I think he thought we'd be just a big bother. So I remember when I was a kid, I thought there wasn't anywhere else to go besides school and Gramma's.

Once in a while when my daddy was drunk, he'd get this big idea that he was gonna take us to the fair that was travelin' through town—so that's where he took us all. Now my mama, well, she had like about eight children, and he decided to take the whole bunch of us. He dumped us there around three in the afternoon in the parking lot, and he took off to go his own way; he left my mama to walk around with all us kids and not a single dime did he give her. Of course, all us children would pull at her and beg for any food at those booths. All the stuff like corn dogs and popcorn—it smelled too good—and so we'd beg, "Please let us get something to eat" and "Please just let us ride just one ride." I remember wantin' just one ticket for one ride. I remember we was there for the whole evenin', and my daddy was nowhere around. That was his pattern—he'd take us somewhere, he'd dump us, and he would just leave. It was totally tormentin' to our mama.

I remember we was there wantin' to eat somethin' or ride any ride, and it got to be like twelve o'clock midnight; Daddy was still gone. There was nobody left, and it was just us wanderin' around. We was cryin', my mama was cryin', and we was just lookin' around the grounds tryin' to decide where to go and how to get home. The man who ran the merry-go-round, well, he saw us and took pity on us, so he let us have just one ride. That's the only ride I ever rode as a child. Really, I think that guy let us ride 'cause he was hopin' we'd ride and leave so he could get home.

I guess we just started walkin' home, and somebody had mercy and picked us up—that must be what happened. Can you 'magine a woman tryin' to walk home with all those tired, hungry children who was all worn out after bein' at a fair all day? She was just tormented and she couldn't even see good, and, well, who's gonna pick up a woman with eight kids? Anyway, somebody, I guess, must have helped us somehow to get back home. Times like these kept me knowin', even as a small child, that someone needed to be in charge of us besides our parents.

Daddy did the same thing to us at Christmas parades. I remember at one event there was all this music and all this live entertainment on the street, and, of course, there'd be drinkin' involved, which Daddy looked for. He didn't just take us to parades in our town; instead, he'd take us to parades in lots of other towns, and each time, he'd totally abandon us and the same thing would happen. We'd walk around with our mama, just her and us—and we'd beg our mama for somethin' to eat or money to buy somethin', and she couldn't provide it. Late at night, our daddy just wouldn't be there.

Other times, when there was not an event to leave us at, he'd take us to some people he knew—people that didn't really like us or want us there. One person in particular was his cousin, or some other relative who would sit and make music with Daddy. Really, my daddy was very talented. But he'd always get started drinkin', then get totally drunk, and then he'd disappear.

Oftentimes he and his cousin would leave, and there we'd be, stuck at his cousin's house with the wife who didn't want us. It'd be all night, and we'd be layin' all over the floor hungry, cold, and uncomfortable. I remember these relatives where he'd leave us. These people would never feed us, of course, and they probably dreaded us comin' 'cause there was a lot of us and times were tough. We was not shown any hospitality at all. They didn't want us there, and I think they thought if they was nice to us, we might come back or somethin'.

Well, even as bad as home was, we wanted to get back there 'cause we knew we belonged there and we was okay at home, or at least it sometimes felt like we was wanted. Back then, my mama called me a "house cat" 'cause I didn't want to go anywhere. Anyway, these kind of memories and things are the reason that right now I hate fairs, parades, and stayin' anywhere. I would beg, "Please don't go with him, Mama. You know what's gonna happen." Still, she would go draggin' her brood behind her for another miserable adventure. No wonder now, I don't like travelin'—I like just bein' home.

The Flood

When I was little and lived in Convict Holler, I was in a flood; I'm not sure, but I think it was about 1977 and I was about ten years old. I remember the old house where we lived; the foundation was made from stacks and stacks of rocks. I remember it rained for days and we was all standin' on the porch in this house and the water was comin' up closer and closer to our house. Suddenly the water started comin' up around the rocks. The water rose higher, and then next the water was up in the house and we were all standin' in water that was cold and muddy lookin'. I remember askin' my mama if we could go swimmin' 'cause it'd been easy to just jump off the porch.

We didn't know the rushin' water had currents that could pull us away. I knew my mama was afraid, but I didn't understand why. I thought it was almost entertainin' to see people's houses, trailers, vehicles, toys, doghouses, 'frigerators, and other belongin's floatin' by our door and we was just standin' there. I don't know if people died from that flood, but I'm sure some did. It musta been God's hand that kept that little house from floatin' off those rocks 'cause most houses in our town was swept away.

I remember the National Guard came to a community nearby, and someone told us that if we went there, they'd give us stuff, good stuff, like disaster kits. Of course, we all went to the shelter, and we each got a kit. It was great! It had a toothbrush—the first toothbrush I ever had—and a blanket, plus even some food. I really can't remember for sure, but I do think that the blanket seemed old and wooly and scratchy, but it kept us warm—and that was a gift 'cause in the country we got so cold. In fact, I recall lots o; times bein' so miserably cold that it hurt. Once I was tryin' to sleep under a mattress to get warm. It didn't work too good 'cause them mattresses was way too heavy and I almost got squished. Plus the mattress didn't stick close or fold down 'round me enough to keep me warm. Anyway, we all appreciated the free gifts we got 'cause o' that flood, and we was so glad the water didn't wash us off.

My Daddy

Around the time of the flood, we was sick a lot. My daddy, well, he would just leave anytime we had a problem. Even though he had a job, he'd just leave all of us at our house. I think sometimes he musta stayed with different women, or sometimes he'd decide to just go stay with his mama. So, well, he'd abandon us for months at a time, and he was gone again around this time when we was livin' in Convict Holler. Well, like I said, we all got real weak and real sick again—so sick we couldn't hold our heads up except for me and Mama. Normal times, we used to get water from our well, fed by a natural spring, but we all knew bein' sick that we needed pure water. We had a real nice neighbor that would let us use the outside water spigot of her house to fill up milk jugs so we could have decent water. Only problem was that by the time I could make it home with them jugs, my hands would be achin'—but still, I was proud to do somethin' for my family. I knew these people also had a phone. So this time when we all was so sick, I convinced Mama that we should call Gram-ma and maybe she could find our daddy and tell him to come help. Why my mama never asked for help for us, I will never know. It's like she just accepted whatever happens, happens.

So me and my mama left the rest of the family laying home sick as could be, and we started to walk to go find water for all us kids and to call for help. The snow was deep and we didn't have proper shoes, boots, or clothes, but still me and my mama started walkin' down that road feelin' so sick and weak. I know for sure that while goin' to that house, we must have fell every two to three feet. We would walk, fall, and walk more until we finally made it somewhere for usin' a phone. We told my gram-ma to tell our daddy that we was all real bad sick and if he didn't come home and do somethin', we could probably all die. I don't remember if he came and can't even remember walkin' home or if anyone came to help. I think it musta been the grace of God that somehow we was kept goin'; I just know that somehow we didn't die, and eventually, somehow we all got well again. Rememberin' how bad this time was in my mind, all I knew for sure was that my daddy, well, he was just never there when we needed him. Still, God pulled us through somehow.

Even as bad as it was at times, I don't hate my daddy. I'd hear stories about how he was abused as a child, and he told all these stories about how he had to quit school in the third grade and go to work plowin' fields for fifty cents a day. But, you know, I don't have to try hard to feel sorry for that boy when he was little. Still, it's harder to feel sorry for the man who didn't step up and do his job as a daddy. It may not have been his purpose, but as a child, it felt like he made it his goal in life to torment us children. It is so sad 'cause he seemed to have great compassion and love for other people but not his own children. So, my daddy, well, he was a poor excuse of a father. That is what he was, but I don't hate him. In fact, I feel bad 'cause nobody told him he should've done better—not one person. He just kept gettin' away with stuff with no consequences, and that made him worse off day by day. So, really, I'm just tellin' it like I saw it—sad as it is.

There was this one place we lived that my daddy actually built close to our gram-ma. It was a small little house. He bought materials and did the work hisself—it was the first house-type place that was really ours. It basically was just a box, and it never had built-in walls and it wasn't ever finished on the outside. It was made of plywood and two-by-fours and whatever he could get. But still we lived in this house, and we loved bein' close to Gram-ma. Sometimes I could go get her to calm my daddy down when he went on a rampage. One day I remember bringin' Gram-ma over to see what Daddy brought home: a microwave oven. I think somebody musta told him about the new technology or somethin', so he brought this oven home and we was all fascinated with it. We didn't have hardly any food to cook in it, but I remember thinking, "Wow, we're rich; we got a microwave!"

The Stand

While livin' in this house, I remember Daddy was so violent when he'd get drunk; those were the times when Daddy would do his best to demolish things. Well burned in my memory, there was this one evenin' when Daddy, he went on a violent streak, so Mama took the kids and went to Gram-ma's. I stayed at home 'cause I thought I was gonna protect our belongin's—I decided to take a stand. Don't know how old I was—I was probably almost eleven or twelve. But I was determined he wasn't breakin' up everything we had. So when he'd go to pull somethin' off to destroy, I tried to get in front of him. He was a big man and I was just a little girl, so I didn't succeed. He'd be throwin' stuff and flailin' his arms, and every time something crashed, I felt like I done let Mama and the other kids down. That night, I remember this little piece of furniture like a dressing table that my gram-ma had gave me, just me, and I loved it. I had lugged it all the way from her house. It had a big round mirror on it and kind of a seat placed in front. I just loved this thing 'cause I liked to sing, and it gave me a spot to sit or stand in front of and sing and sing and watch myself in the mirror. It was kinda like my own stage.

Well, Daddy run out of things to bust up, so he went to my dressin' table and decided to destroy it. I remember standin' in front of my table, and I tried to put my hands up to brace myself in front of it. I really thought I could keep him from breakin' the mirror, so we struggled—he pulled on it and I was pushin' on it. Then suddenly the whole thing just shattered and crashed, cutting my body up in a lot of places. I didn't know my arm was cut deep till blood started pourin' and spurtin' on my foot; suddenly I couldn't feel my fingers or arm anymore. I looked down, and there was this huge gash in my arm and I could see the bone, which had a little bit of fat on it. My daddy stood lookin' at my arm, and I said, "Look what you did . . .

my arm's cut really bad!" Well, the blood was still gushin', and he just mumbled somethin'; really, well, he cussed. Then he just suddenly decided to leave. He ran out the door and up into the woods. Just like he always did, he'd run off when we needed him.

So I had to get to my gramma's house with blood pourin' down my arm; luckily it wasn't too far to get there, but then we still had to get to my aunt and uncle's house. Thank goodness they lived close, and they could take me to the hospital. This time I guess if I hadn't had stitches or somethin', I probably woulda bled to death 'cause that wound was deep and huge. Seems amazin', but I remember my mama tryin' to help me to get my story straight. So, I made up some lie just like my mama told me to. I was so angry at my daddy for doin' this and at my mama for makin' me lie 'bout it. Now I have this big scar on my arm. It don't bother me much 'cause I'm not a movie star, but now when I look down at my arm, I see a constant reminder of my childhood, and a little sadness starts to creep into my everyday life.

Time to Laugh

I want to talk about some funny things that happened about this time when I was growin' up. Us kids was always findin' a way to try to have fun, and someone discovered a small place to play games under the front porch floor. You know, like when a floor has spaces between the slats, some of us kids would be standin' on the deck, and we could see the others who would be playin' cards or some game, usually by invitation only. They'd be hoggin' the game all to themselves. One of my older left-out siblin's decided it would be funny to pee on the porch floor right above the ones playin', and sure enough, it worked! With a little aim, my brother, well, he could manage to hit the target every time. It was actually funny as long as you was with the group that was doing the peein'!

I remember there was a time my daddy was helpin' neighbors kill a hog—often neighbors saw this as "helpin'" each other. And I guess the people thought they was bein' nice and they rewarded us with the hog's head. And a hog's head is a lot to work with and a lot to mess with if you want to try and eat it—plus there's not a lot o' meat or anything for your efforts. So my mama—well, she didn't like these people my daddy helped, so she told my sister Theresa and me to get rid of the hog's head before my daddy came home. So Theresa grabbed one ear and I grabbed the other; it's gross but I remember he was still warm. We walked out and tried to decide where to put it. Well, I don't know why with all them woods available all 'round our house, but we chose to just walk out to the outdoor toilet, lift up a couple boards of the floor in the corner, and put the hog's head in the space under them boards. Well, the hog's head wouldn't fit all the way down in there. In fact, it was like stickin' up with the boards on top of it—so, from then on for 'bout a year, we had to go to the bathroom with a scary old hog lookin' at us. Thank goodness that hogs head slowly disappeared as it changed to dust. It was such a dumb idea that we had; I remember we just always tried to see it as funny. 'Cause our toilet stunk real bad, most times we hardly noticed the added stench of the hog's head. But for sure, we noticed them eyes lookin' at us.

Then one time, I got mad at my brother Roy 'cause he used to hang my doll up in a tree and shoot it with his BB gun. I still don't know where he got that gun. Well, someone had made me a sock doll, and he'd hang it up in the tree and shoot it while I stood there and cried. Guess he learned this from his daddy. Well, Roy only had one pair of shoes, and I got so mad I threw one of his shoes in the toilet. And it was really nasty in there. Some people would pour lye or some kind of chemical in their outhouse to keep it nice, but ours was always really gross and nasty, with creepy things crawlin' around. I remember my daddy gettin' mad at me, and he told me I had to get the boot out of the toilet hole and then I had to wash it off. So, I got me a long stick and fished that dang boot out; I took it and throwed it in the creek and sloshed it around a little, which didn't do a real good cleanin' job, but it was the best I could do keepin' my distance. Anyway, lookin' back, Roy was pretty mad, but I thought that was funny.

Then there was a time about in the fourth or fifth grade when my brother Ray was kind of like assigned to me to take care of. Well, Ray slept with us, and of course, we all slept together. One night when Ray was a baby and was still wearin' diapers, I think that he had on one of those cloth diapers, the kind that could slide off pretty easy. That's exactly what happened: Ray's diaper musta slid off, and he pooped in my hair—and I had really long stringy hair. Realizin' the problem in the morning, I was determined I was goin' to school anyway. Problem was that we had zero detergent of any kind—no washin' detergent, no body soap, no dish detergent, no shampoo—we had nothing, nothing to wash my hair!

My sisters rinsed my hair out as good as they could with plain water, but there wasn't nothin' they could do without soap to really clean-wash it. Everybody said, "You can't go to school" and "You stink real bad," but I was determined about not missin' school. So I got a bright idea: I put a ski hat on my head; you know, one of those old long ones that had a tassel on the end of it. I thought it was pretty, and I called it my toboggan. The only problem was that it was summertime—it didn't matter to me 'cause I was still determined I was goin' to school, where they had lunch. And go to school I did! I had to fend off people all day sayin' things and tryin' to yank the cap off my head. I'm sure I stank 'cause kids, they were sayin' they could smell somethin' bad through the hat. Then, bein' curious, they'd ask, "Why you wearin' that ski cap?" They just wouldn't leave me alone. It was pretty bad 'cause my hair was still wet under that toboggan, and I remember my head bein' kept warm under that toboggan. Well, it started to get really itchy—in fact, it itched all day. I thought it was pretty funny that I had to go to school in the summertime with a toboggan on my head—guess I had my sense of humor, and that helped.

I remember one time when Mom and Dad was gone. In fact, all the bigger people were gone. I was little, and we was hungry. I had not a clue on how to bake bread. But since we was all hungry, I was determined to fix somethin' and thought that I knowed how to fix bread with flour, water, and bakin' sodi. So I put a whole can of sodi in a bowl with about four cups o' flour and enough water to make it stick together. No surprise that it came out flat as a paper. Never bein' short on tellin' stories, I told my siblin's that this was called "Chinese bread," and, you know, they believed it and they ate it! We woulda thought anything was good at that time, and it eased the pain o' hunger.

Oops!

One day I was watchin' TV, and I saw a beautiful, blond-headed girl draw on some real pretty eyebrows with a pencil. I got an idea—I was always gettin' ideas that I never cleared with anybody. So, that night when everybody was sleepin', I sneaked out of bed as quiet as a mouse and got my daddy's razor. See, I knew for sure from experience that if us kids could fall asleep in over-crowded beds after hearin scary stories and walkin four to five miles each day, there was no wakin us up easy. So, by the light of the moon shinin' through the window, I figured I was safe to shave off the first set of eyebrows

I came to—and they just happened to belong to my sister Missy. There she was with no eyebrows, and it hit me then that I didn't have one o' them eyebrow pencils. So I sort of wished I had thought the whole thing through, but it was too late. I really did feel bad for what I did, but it was already done and I couldn't see how a confession on my part would improve the situation.

Well, I put my daddy's razor back where I got it and crawled back into bed. I woke up the next morning to hear my sister Teresa, who was sleeping in between me and Missy, say, "Missy, you ain't got no eyebrows." We all gathered around and looked on as Missy felt around on her face tryin' to find her eyebrows, with me lookin' just as shocked as the rest of my siblin's. We all went to tell our mama about it, and she was doing somethin' in the kitchen. I remember my poor little mama threw up her hands in the air and said, "Lord, have mercy—these children done caught somethin' that makes your eyebrows fall out!" We was all so glad that it only happened to Missy, with me being ever so thankful I was never found out. I confessed when we was grown, but *not* until then.

God's Hands and Feet: Grace through People

Teachers

When we was growin' up, you know there was some people that were always so kind to us. I remember that at Christmas time they'd have all the poor kids come to the cafeteria, and they'd have Santa in there and kids usually got somethin' like *Checkers* or *Chutes and Ladders* or *Parcheesi*—somethin' like that. Usually once every year, I remember each of us, we'd get somethin' at the poor kids party. Then there were also class parties where we were supposed to bring a gift for the kid who's name we drew. Me and my siblings, we never had money for buyin gifts. So it was kinda sad when the other kids were excited to get someone's name, to bring their surprise gift, and to open some mystery gift for them. What a blessing that my teachers always had somethin wrapped up for me – even if it was just some plain, used kind of clothes or toys. It still looked like I was gettin somethin and takin part in the party fun. Turns out most all my siblings' teachers got presents for them, too, and we all appreciated how those teachers covered for us.

Church People

I remember sometimes when it was Christmas or Thanksgiving holidays, there'd be somebody to show up with a box of food—it was wonderful! So I tell people all the time, "When you think that you might be doing a food bank or you are trying to help by giving good food to people who don't have much, and you start bein' tempted to maybe think that it's not a big deal or why bother? Well, believe me—it *is* a big deal to some little kid who hasn't had a meal like that in a while." It was a huge deal to us. It was the best part of holiday and celebratin' times, and I'm still grateful!

Dr. Slewenski's Office

I remember one good time when we were little, and this was after we moved to Statesvillle, North Carolina, and I didn't actually live with my family; instead, I lived with the neighbors. My daddy and Mama called me home and told me that there was this eye doctor, and every year his family and office workers, they did somethin' nice for a family. This year these people decided to do somethin' for our family. My daddy said, "Now I want to know what you want for Christmas." I just couldn't 'magine—I'd never been asked what I wanted for Christmas or any other occasion. I had no idea how to pick somethin' or how to act when I learned we'd be gettin' somethin' from people we didn't know. I tried to be practical 'cause

I didn't think we'd really get anything anyway. Finally I said, "I'd like to have a pair of boots." Problem was that all my siblin's were smart and they said they knew this thing was real, so each one, they made lists, which led to gifts like each boy gettin' a bicycle, my sister Theresa gettin' a tape recorder with a bunch of tapes, and my sister Melissa gettin' a baby doll with tons of outfits, baby furniture, baby clothes, and other stuff. Then there was me; I only got one pair of boots 'cause that's all I asked for. But to see all our family with all their presents—it was awesome anyway. The doctor's name was Dr. Slewenski, and he was in Statesville, North Carolina. I'll never forget what that family and his office people did for my family.

There were other times when church people would give us stuff at Christmas. All these were times of grace, and I just won't never forget these people. I also won't forget a valuable lesson: Now when my Heavenly Father asks me, "Karen, what do you want?" I'm quick to tell him everything on my heart, even if it's a long list. I know He wants to bless His children, and I know He will do what's best.

Mr. Hess

I guess everybody has their stories about how hard they had it and stuff, but I appreciate everything everybody done for us and I'll never forget any of the blessings. Like when we knew Mr. Hess, a teacher who was also the bus driver and the principal at Harmon Elementary, where we kids went. I remember that we were ridin' the bus on the last day of school before Christmas vacation, and Mr. Hess, he let everybody off the bus but he didn't let us off at our stop. I thought, "Hey, this is really weird." At first I was worried: maybe he was a strange perv or somebody who was goin' to kidnap us or abuse us or somethin', and that would mean we'd be taken from our family again. But when he finally did stop that bus, he had some great presents for each one of us. I got a coat! Thanks, Mr. Hess! That coat kept me warm—I even slept in it!

Andy Manard

Same kind a thing happened with a church bus driver; his name was Andy Manard. He came to drive a church bus up in the holler to get us 'cause of my sister Mary. See, all of my siblin's left home as soon as they could 'cause, I may have already said this, but when someone worked hard, people wanted you to stay with them and help with their children and housework and such and we were all hard workers. So each of my older sisters found families and got out; it was so on down the line.

Mary started stayin' with another family, and she was goin' to church with them. Sometimes she'd make sure that the church bus driver would come get us even though I think that he wasn't supposed to drive to our holler 'cause the road was *bad*—really *bad*. If the people at the church had known where he was takin' that nice church bus, he woulda had real problems. I can remember the scrapin' and scratchin' sounds of the rocks and holes as the bus bottom moved over huge ruts in the roads, and the creeks he had to turn around in—they was a total dangerous mess. I remember ridin' there one night in particular. This night they weren't gonna have regular church, and instead we walked out to a revival tent, where they was worshippin' instead of in the church buildin'. It was Grace Baptist Church in Grundy, Virginia. The preacher preached on hell, where the rich man and Lazarus died and how the rich man begged for Lazarus to bring just one drop of water for his tongue. The preacher said, "If you're not saved and you die, then you'll go to hell." Well, I wasn't no brain surgeon, but I had enough sense to know that I didn't want to go to hell.

Lookin' back, I always knew that the bus driver went out of his way to come get me—and, well, without him, I wouldn't have got to go to church. And that meant I wouldn't have got saved without him, neither. 'Cause I knew enough to be grateful, I gave my son Jonathan a middle name after the bus driver named Andy, who was so kind and determined to drive that church bus so we could hear about God. My son's name is Jonathan Andrew. It's a constant reminder of the day I asked God to save me and I became His. This didn't change my circumstances, but I knew I could cry out to Him and He would hear. Before that, I wasn't sure anybody heard my pleas for help.

Mama–Socks of Sacrifice

I remember this time in school when we was all excited 'cause in PE we were all gonna get to jump on the new trampoline. I couldn't wait! Except the teacher said, "Bring some socks if you want to jump on the trampoline tomorrow." My heart sank; I felt panic 'cause I didn't have no matchin' socks. All my socks were mismatched, filled with holes, and lookin' bad. Kids always laughed at my socks even when I wore shoes 'cause one was usually navy and one was brown and they was full of pulled threads and stains. After dinner, I mentioned to Mama that some days I wished I had better socks—I just wanted to look like the other children and not get laughed at. I told her I knew what was gonna happen the next day: all the kids was gonna laugh when I took my shoes off. My mama held me tight and told me she was sorry. I think I cried myself to sleep. Next mornin', I dreaded goin' to school, but again, I knew I'd at least get lunch!

So, I got up. Surprised, I found a pair of matchin' socks on the foot of my bed. I couldn't believe it! But quick as a blind dog in a meat house, I snatched those socks up, runnin' into the other room to pull them on—almost afraid someone was gonna take them away. After I was total ready for school, I hurried to get out the door. In the rush, I noticed somethin' hangin' on a chair—there was Mama's only sweater (she had no coat and only one sweater). Anyway, as I stopped to be lookin' more closely, I noticed somethin—the sleeves was missin'. To this day, I'm sad thinkin' of Mama's thin arms goin' bare, but I'm grateful how she gave up her comfort to see I had proper socks and protected feelin's.

The Boyd Family: The Best Week of My Life

Well, I think it musta been after my arm got cut that my mama— well, I'm not sure if it was her retina that was separatin' or if she had real bad cataracts on both eyes, but she could hardly see. I really think her retinas were separatin' in both eyes; it musta been scary for her. Havin' major eye surgery left her with patches on both eyes for days. My oldest sister, Lona, was married and lived in a tiny trailer where the whole bunch of us were all stayin' 'cause Mama couldn't take care of us or do anything, and we sure couldn't take care of her, either. Anyway, while my sister Lona had us, it was wintertime, and I started goin' and spendin' the night with a friend from school named Sharon Boyd.

I remember one special time I had went for a sleepover for one night, but we got snowed in and it became the very best week of my life! Their family was just like the families that you watch on TV: the house was nice, the family was nice to each other, everything was clean, they had food to eat, their mama was a maid, and their daddy worked real hard—he played music and worked in the coal mines. I thought it was the best place in the world; and at the end of that week, I think they got to know me a little bit and I told them about some of the stuff that was going on at home. They began to understand how bad things was. They asked me, "Would you want to stay with us until things get straightened out and ya'll get to go home?" Of course, I said yes.

So, quick I went to Lona's, where my mama, family, and my stuff was; I was gonna just get my belongin's. Course, while I was tellin' them what I was doin', my sister chimed in sayin' she thought it was a great idea, but my mama didn't. My bein' determined and 'cause my mama couldn't do much with patches on her eyes and her needin' drugs and painkillers, altogether it meant I got to stay with the Boyds. And I loved it—it was the best! I went to school clean and neat, and they got me clothes and every kinda supply I could 'magine. I had pencils, paper, markers, a ruler, and other stuff, and it was great. I remember kids comin' up to me and sayin', "Hey, Karen, I like your new style." I guess they thought I just decided all of a sudden to clean up and have the things I never had before. No one other than my family knew that all the good changes in me came from the Boyd's. I stayed with them only a couple months—it was over way too soon.

Difficult People–Difficult Times: The Spoiler

I used to think of my daddy at times like the spoiler—the one who loved to make things hard. I didn't know but found out later that while Mama and the family stayed with Lona, Daddy had called and told them all, "If you don't want to stay at this house that I built, I'll burn it down!" And that's exactly what he did—he burned down the house with everything we had of any value in it, all our belongin's. Everything was all ashes now! Like I said, my family kept the fire a secret till a couple weeks after it had happened. When they told me about the fire, they also started tellin' me the welfare was gonna rent Mama a trailer somewhere in Garden Creek, which was close to Grundy. With all this news, they also let me know that I was gonna have to go stay with the family in Mama's trailer 'cause then she could get more money and help from the welfare. I really, really hated to leave the Boyds, but I had to! And so I did.

The Boyds, they came and got me like every weekend. That special family made me feel like part of their family every single weekend. But I was with Mama and our family for all the school weeks. The welfare had given Mama money, and so we had food on the table, the trailer was clean, we had new clothes, and it was kinda like a normal life and we were lovin' it. We stayed there for a month or two and were enjoyin' the new trailer; everything was goin' good. We didn't know where our daddy was, and we didn't care that he ran off after he burned the house down. So, we didn't even see him for a long time. That month or two—it was so nice.

Then one time I was spendin' a fun weekend with the Boyds, and it was all goin' so normal. Then along came Daddy, showin' up in a truck at the Boyds' house. Mr. Boyd told me, "Your daddy's out there, so you better go out there and see him." I was dreadin' it, but I went, and Daddy said, "Get your sorry ass in this truck, and we're leavin'; we're goin' to North Carolina." My heart sank; it was broken to pieces. I was cryin' so hard, near hysterical, and I was so mad and sad all at the same time, but nothin' could be done.

To this day, I'm grateful that Mr. Phillip Boyd was home that day, and I know this musta took a lot o' guts, but he walked up to that truck and he looked straight into my daddy's eyes and said, "If you'll let her stay with us, I'll bring her to visit anytime you want."

"No, Karen's goin' with me," was Daddy's fast words.

So there I stood. Part of me feelin' so sad 'cause I was gonna have to leave these people who actually wanted me. But another part of me—well, it was kinda surprisin' and kinda weird, 'cause I felt happy inside. See, before this, in my mind, *no one* had *ever* wanted me. Seein' Mr. Phillip Boyd standin' there with tears in his eyes askin' my daddy to let me stay with him and his family, well, it made me feel wanted for the first time in my life, and I'll never forget it! Plus, I'll never forget how they was so good to me. They treated me like one of their own.

Another Move–Another Hard Time

And so we began our trip to North Carolina. We traveled there with everything that we had crammed into the back of our truck and a van. Most of the kids, we rode in the back of the van; it was like one of those used for, well, you know, like haulin' businesses' stuff or whatever. I remember clearly that in this van, there was many belongin's plus there were also bees. Four big beehives were stuck in one corner and covered by some thick sheets or quilts. It's amazin' that we didn't even worry about the fact that if we'd got hit by a car or in a wreck, all those bees woulda been all over us—they woulda stung us to death. As for me, I didn't have energy to worry about much 'cause I was just upset and sad to be leaving the family who liked me and shared with me such a normal, amazin' life.

In North Carolina, we moved to my brother-in-law's house. This house had gotten moved from a site after a friend told him, "If you can get this house out o' here, you can have it." So somehow he'd gotten that house jacked up and gotten it onto some kind o' trailer and moved it to our new location. You can 'magine how if you move a house without a professional, it can really mess up that house. So, even though he managed to move the house, it was barely standin' straight on his property in Stoney Point, North Carolina—a very small, backwards town. They kept tryin' to level it by puttin' some blocks under the floor. The roof was all tore up 'cause o' the movin', so they patched up the holes as best they could. Anyway, it didn't have electricity or water 'cause it didn't meet building codes. And well, I didn't think we'd ever get that stuff done so we could hook up utilities. I was right; we just kept livin' there with no electric or water. So, once again, we went to school dirty and hungry every day.

Well, it was in this messed-up house we stayed with my sister and her husband and her little boy and whatever druggies, bums, and drunks wanted to come; and, well, I think my brother-in-law was a drug dealer, and that's why there were so many homeless abusers all around. And I remember sleepin' by strangers and then wakin' up next to people I didn't know. Each mornin' I'd have to step over these strange people to go anywhere. It was so awful to live with so many people I didn't know. We just all slept anywhere we could find a spot on the floor. My heart went back and forth, from fear to sadness, from fear to sadness.

What Doesn't Kill You

Another one of the worst days of my life happened around this time in the seventh grade. A girl in my class had parents who were feudin' with my family; I never knew why they was arguin', but I knew their daughter was really mad at me for some reason that I didn't understand. This girl, she started gossipin' to my only friend and makin' her mad at me by telling her untrue stories. Things got bad enough that everyone told my friend to fight me at second recess time; I didn't want to fight but somehow knew I had no choice. The whole class was knowin' what was comin' that day. After we got out to the recess area, everyone circled around this girl and me, and she started hittin' me. Since I didn't want to or know how to fight, she hurt me real bad. But that wasn't the worst thing. I remember like it was yesterday: these kids were chantin', "Kick her in the face, pull her hair, knock her out, hit her in the belly," and stuff like that. I felt like I was surrounded on all sides by a huge circle of kids, and they was all shoutin' that they hated me. *No one* was pullin' for me, not *no one*! You just can't 'magine, but this can make for a real heavy heart. So I learned that what doesn't kill you—well, it makes you know you can make it through almost anything. You just have to keep pressin' on and keep goin'; you don't never give up. Knowin' these things got me back to school the next day and helped me get through tough times later. But I'll tell you the truth, I'll never forget that awful, awful day.

Invisible at Home, Target at School

This was one of the hardest times of my life 'cause we went to a new school and we was poor and dirty and everyone knew it; so, of course, it caused people to laugh at us. I remember I was in the seventh grade when I could just 'bout feel the gossipin'. I was so hungry 'cause we didn't have no food at home. No adults in the house were sober, ever, startin' from the first day we had moved to Stoney Point, North Carolina. That's how it was. The people livin' in our house, they found a doctor who would write prescription drugs, and they had all that supply, plus marijuana, beer, and liquor—so they stayed drugged and drunk all the time. We had no food, but they had drugs and booze.

I remember bein' so hungry at this new school, and I think I got free lunch somehow. Guess it was 'cause I always filled out the applications for all us kids. I'd just make up numbers and sign my mama's name. One day when I came to sit at the table, two girls came and sat close at my table. Both girls watched me eat every bite of food, and one said, "If she licks that spoon, I'll throw up." I thought in my mind maybe I wouldn't eat it all just to pretend that I wasn't too hungry, but of course I changed my mind.

I remember most every day always bein' made fun of and picked on, and this was a *really* bad time. I hated North Carolina at this time, and I started hatin' all the adults that was supposed to be takin' care of us. When things got unbearable and gosh-awful, I remember sayin' to God:

"God, I knelt in those wood shavin's at that revival.

I asked you to save me—I'm yours now,

so I'm askin' you to help me *now*!"

Well, God did help. He sent me one person who seemed safe, kind, and sensitive to me at school—in fact, he was the biggest blessin' I can remember at that school. His name was Coach Moore, and he was a teacher and sports coach at Stoney Point Junior High School. About ten thirty in the mornin', he'd walk by my desk after deliverin' snacks to each student; on his second trip around, he'd place an extra carton of milk on my desk. Every day he'd say, "Well, I had an extra one today." Lookin' back, I know he had to be orderin' that extra milk to provide more for me 'cause he knew how much I needed it.

God also gave me Mary at this time. I used to walk to a pay phone and call her a lot. Mary was quick to tell me to pick up a phone anytime I needed help; she'd be there to answer. Well, that turned out to be 'bout three or four times every week. She'd always take my collect calls and I bet it cost her a lot, but she never mentioned it. There wasn't much she could do to help with my bad livin' situation 'cause she was a newlywed and she lived in Virginia. But she always had a scripture and one of God's encouragin' words to share with me. I knew I had to fend for myself, but it helped to know God and Mary, they was on my side.

I used to walk with my mama to a store close to a mile away where she had a charge account. It was like a beer joint and liquor store combo, but it also sold bologna and bread. Sometimes I could talk her into charging bread and bologna so we would have somethin' to eat. That's what we kids ate when we could get it: loaf bread and bologna. Actually, that's what I ate for at least a year when

I was thirteen. It was a sad time. The men stayin' with us gave me a lot of attention and I don't know how I didn't get raped. It sure coulda happened 'cause I didn't know not to put myself in dangerous situations. I don't know why I was protected, but it musta been God! And I thank Him!

Another House, Another School, Another Trial

Next we found an abandoned house in Statesville, so we moved again—meanin', once again, we started another new school. I remember it was so bad bein' in a poor, broken-down house somewhere new facin' a new school with new kids to pick on us. I had a blue room there, and the house had four bedrooms total. In the livin' room, it did have a stove, but, of course, we didn't have no food to cook on it. Problem was, we didn't use it for heat neither, and I remember it was so cold we'd be hurtin'. Some of the windows, they was missin', so my family just taped up pieces of tin over them. My parents just kept gettin' worse and worse as far as drinkin' and smokin' pot. They was gracious to all the bums and drunks that had lived in Stoney Point, so they'd follow us and use our home as their home.

It was here that my sister, who was fifteen, ended up gettin' pregnant by one of these creeps. He was an old guy with a bald head, and I don't totally blame him. I don't think my sister ever knew his name, but I remember that he was from Michigan. My daddy never stepped up, protected us, or took any responsibility for this happenin' to my sister, and I couldn't help blamin' him. He was supposed to be takin' care of us. He just didn't seem to know how to care like a daddy should. The anger I felt over this was almost consumin'.

At school I think they found out about Theresa bein' pregnant, and they tried to offer her help; but, instead, my parents got in touch with my Aunt Dot, who had always wanted a child. Theresa, it seemed, wasn't aware what was goin' on. See, she had learnin' disabilities and was in special education at the time. So, she agreed to go stay with Dot and have the baby, not aware it was for Dot to adopt. I know that must have been so hard for my sister.

With Theresa gone, I found a girl who was my age in the neighborhood, and somehow I spent a lot o' time with her family. I worked for them by housekeeping, and I got to stay with them at nights. I cried myself to sleep at night 'cause I felt bad not bein' with my younger siblin's. One night I was goin' to a youth rally with them, and the lady of the home, Margie, said, "Karen, I have to take you to your sister's house . . . somethin' awful has happened." I knew that my family got in dumpsters to look for usable stuff, and I knew there was broken glass, sharp stuff, and lots to hurt them. So I was really worried, thinkin' maybe someone got injured or got run over tryin' to get to the dumpster.

Margie said she couldn't tell me what had happened. I felt so bad; I was almost hysterical. This woman who worked in a home close by had some pills, so she gave me some kind of nerve pill. Maybe I shouldn't have taken them pills, but it might have been a good thing 'cause when I got there and saw my family sittin' there, I almost collapsed. They told me that it was my brother Roy. He'd got killed in a car crash, and I just couldn't believe it. My heart was broke. Roy was only eighteen years old. Part of me was grateful that it wasn't the little ones gone, but my brother Roy had helped us and took care of us, and he was just beautiful. I couldn't believe he was gone.

When I was around fourteen and my brother Roy died I was feelin' kinda depressed, so I went and lived with the Byrd family in Statesville. While I was stayin' with them, my own family bought a nice home. Roy had a small life insurance policy from where he worked and the settlement after his death allowed for mama to put money down on a house. It was the first time my family had money for a nice house in a nice neighborhood, so I decided to go spend the summer with them in Taylorville. That's where I met one of the older potheads who drank with my sister May and with my daddy. This guy, he was twenty, and I was only fourteen; I won't mention his name. My daddy did not protect his children, and he allowed me to go anywhere with my sister and this guy. Well, as you might 'magine, now I see this man as a predator. I think from the very beginning, he planned on taking advantage of a young, naive girl like me, and I don't know how I wound up okay. I regret that time, but I'm okay now. For sure, you live and you learn.

A New Beginnin'—Terry Bell

Anyway, this older pothead, he started runnin' from the law and plain disappeared; that's when I agreed to go out with Terry Bell, one of the guys on the block. He was clean-cut, with pretty blue eyes, handsome, and he liked me. He was two years older than me and I liked older guys, but I was glad that he was at least close to my age. Anyway, he was good to me and, actually, he knew the way to my heart. See, at this time, we were still in the nice house, but we didn't have no food, nice furniture, or much stuff inside. We still had the same daddy, who didn't buy groceries much so there wasn't hardly anything to eat.

Terry, he was sixteen, and he worked at a grocery store. Soon he figured out our situation. So after he got off work, he would stop by our house and give me, my sisters, and my brothers food. I thought, *Hmmm—this ain't so bad*, and I figgered I'd start datin' him. He was just so sweet and so kind, and that made me feel better since I was already, well, I already felt like used merchandise. Guess I was promiscuous, but Terry, he just kept comin' back, so I dated him along with other people. He stayed interested in me no matter how much I hurt his feelin's by seein' other people. He'd come back again and again, and he told me that he loved me. He kept bringin' food and bein' good to my family. I always said I could not shake him off even when I was really mean to him.

I had in the meantime moved to Statesville to live with the Moore's, another family willing to take me into their home. They was good to me but at this time I was actin' rebellious about school and rules and such. So I wore out my welcome there kinda quick. Terry, he knew I needed a place to live, so he was determined we'd get married at this very young age. He talked his mom into letting me stay at their house, and I roomed with his two sisters. I was only sixteen, and I knew that if I kept screwin' around I was gonna get pregnant, so I decided to stay out of school and go with a lady friend to the doctor. We went to the health department, and they gave me a great big supply of stuff. It was a big brown paper bag full of foam, condoms, and birth control pills. They told me, "As soon as you start your period, you need to start the pills the Sunday after." Well, I never started, and I wasn't sure what to do. Bein' so young, I figgered I better get back to the health department. I asked them, "Should I just take the pills anyway?" They said they needed to examine me, and the exam was so embarrassin' and shockin' 'cause that's how I found out I was pregnant. That day I was so devastated; my only thought was, *How can I be a mama? I'm not even good at bein' a teenager.* Since Terry had been the only guy constant in my life and he was the only one that I was sexually active with, well, I knew that the baby, it was his. I kept thinkin', *What have I done to an innocent child?*

Doin' What I Had To

So I lived with Terry's family, even though his mama didn't like me—and I don't blame her, 'cause I wasn't what you would want for a daughter-in-law. She agreed to let me stay there for a little while. I told Terry and his mom about the day at the clinic and how I had to be helped out to the car by this lady 'cause I was so upset and devastated. I cried for a long, long time. But Terry, who was only eighteen, well, I think he was happy about all this. I think he knew now I couldn't go anywhere after this 'cause I was his now. He just decided we was gettin' married, and since I had no other plans and no way out, that's what I did. About a month later, we got married at his mother's house. We was real poor, so I borrowed a dress. It wasn't even a real weddin' dress; it was just kind o' cream colored.

I look back now at that day when I got married at sixteen, and it was a pretty good day. We got married in my husband's mama's livin' room, and all the relatives who could be there had come. Because it was such a little livin' room, we were really, really close to the preacher when we were facin' him. He held the Holy Bible in his hand, and he had us repeat stuff. I remember I was so nervous that my knees actually banged against each other. I was standin' there and my hands were shakin' and my palms were sweaty. I thought I should run, just run out the door. I knew I shouldn't get married 'cause I knew I didn't love this guy. I thought maybe he loved me and wanted to take care of me, so I didn't know no other way. So I just went ahead and got married while I was hearin' a big voice in my head sayin', "Don't do it."

Not the Best Time for Panic

Me and Terry's Wedding Nov 12, 1983
16 and 18 years old; borrowed dress

So, like I said, I was all shaky the whole weddin' ceremony. While the preacher was talkin' and we was standin' 'bout eight inches from him, I knew he could hear my knees knockin' real fast and hard. Plus I was feelin' so trapped, knowin' I shouldn't be gettin' married, but feelin' like I had to; the conflict made me discover somethin' weird about myself. Seems that when I get frightened, real upset, or real emotional, sometimes I start gigglin' kind of out o' control. I know there's a medical term for it, and I'm not the only one who does "hysterical laughter" when they feel stressed. That's what I did when my husband started sayin' his vows; I started lookin' at his face, and I busted out laughin'! I knew in my heart and my mind that I should not be laughin', but I could not hold it in no matter how hard I tried. I started spittin' and sniffin' and snortin' all over the place; and the preacher, who probably had doubts that he should be marryin' a couple that was only sixteen and eighteen years old anyway, he started lookin' at me kind o' mean. In fact, everybody 'round us was lookin' at me kind o' mean and disgusted, but I just couldn't stop it.

I laughed all through our weddin', and it hurt my husband's feelin's; in fact, he never really forgot or forgave it. He didn't understand that it really was somethin' I couldn't stop. It's happened since then; once when I was in real bad pain, I did it. I figger everybody has somethin' weird about themselves, and this is mine. So that's what I did on my weddin' day, and I kind of feel, well, for that, I feel real sorry. Still, I wish everyone who'd seen me actin' so weird on that day had known there weren't nothin' I could do to prevent feelin' hysterical. Puttin' it simple, I didn't have no experience handlin' emotions strong as those was.

After the weddin', we had cake, and it was a pretty cake that his aunt had made. On our honeymoon, we went to the grocery store, and for me that was great; I loved it. We bought some food, cooked it up, and stayed in. There we sat on our old, nylon-covered couch. We were so young it was fun to just stay up late and watch TV all night. I know that doesn't sound very exciting or romantic, but we'd managed to start livin in our own house, one that was supposed to be both mine and Terry's and nobody could tell us to leave. That's what I kept thinkin', and so I kept pokin' my husband and sayin', "Are we really married? Are we really married? Can you believe we are really married?" I couldn't believe it! Anyway, Terry had the day off on Sunday to sleep in, but he had to go back to work on Monday.

Reality Sets In

So we was livin' in this little trailer that my husband had bought for four thousand dollars, which meant he was in big debt. To earn more, Terry left the grocery store and he got a job workin at Craftmasater Furniture Company on an assembly line upholstering furniture. In no time he was made the line leader. There's an old sayin', "The cream always rises to the top." I believe it. He kept workin' really, really hard, and he was a smart man. He put every dime of his money that he got paid toward our trailer bill, food, power, and stuff. We barely made it, I tell you for sure. We wasn't married very long when I needed to start goin' to the doctor 'cause of the baby comin'. We didn't get no help from any social services or whatever, and we had no insurance and no way to pay the eight hundred dollars up front. The doctor required us to pay a bunch o' the money in advance, and it took every dime. It was a really hard time. We ate beans every day, which was good for me bein' pregnant. I didn't work at this time 'cause nobody wanted to hire pregnant girls. I felt like deadweight on my husband.

Anyway, I tried to make our little trailer a home. On our first Christmas, 'cause I didn't have much in my kitchen, Terry got me a lot o' kitchen stuff for my personal gifts. This hurt my feelin's real bad. I bought him a basketball. How was I supposed to know that it was plastic? Well, *he* sure knew it and never let up tellin' me about leather bein' better. Guess I hurt his feelin's about as bad as possible. So, that was our first kinda disappointin' Christmas, and from then on we just settled in and worked hard.

Kristina–June 6, 1984

Kristina Marie Bell
beautiful and smart

Well, by the grace of God, Terry took real good care o' me while I was pregnant. I didn't work outside the home, but I tried real hard to cook and clean the way I thought the "normal" families did. I did okay for most of the pregnancy, but when I was seven months along,

I went for a regular checkup. I remember I'd been real dizzy, but I thought that was normal for bein' pregnant. The nurse came in and checked my blood pressure, and then she checked it again. She ran out and got the doctor, and he checked my blood pressure one more time. He said I had to go to the hospital and that I had a condition called toxemia. He said if my blood pressure was not down in the morning, I would have an emergency C-section and my child would be born early. I was so afraid for my little one. When I was alone that evenin' in the hospital bed, I cried out to my Lord sayin,

"Remember me, the girl who knelt in the wood shavin's?

Please help me now."

And *He* did!

The next morning my blood pressure was down and I got to go home. I was put on bed rest, but I didn't really understand what that meant. So I took it a little easier, but I still cooked and cleaned. I figgered if Terry was supportin' me, the least I could do was have supper waitin' for him when he got home. I had to go for a stress test every other day after that. But we was able to hold off for delivery. Kristina was born only two weeks early by a C-section on June 6, 1984. *Thank You, Jesus!*

I planned on breast-feeding and using cloth diapers 'cause that was the cheapest way to go. While at the hospital recoverin' from my C-section, my milk came in real fast while I was nursin' Kristina—and all of a sudden she almost strangled to death. I had pulled the sleeves of my hospital gown off to nurse her, and then she started to choke. I buzzed the buzzer for the nursery—but no one came. Kristina was turnin' black and blue in my arms. I jumped out o' bed, laid her down, and ran in the bathroom naked as a jaybird so I could pull the emergency chain. A big alarm went off, and nurses and doctors and such filled the room. I stood horrified as I watched them revive my little girl. They got the milk from her lungs, and she began to breathe normally. It was only then that I realized that I was naked in front of like twenty people; I was wearin' only feminine protection and a weird elastic belt to hold it into place. I didn't even care—my baby was okay—*Thank You, Jesus!*

I blamed myself for this, and I cried until my face was raw. I went to the nursery to feed her after that for the rest of the hospital stay. I was so nervous the day I took her home. I had just turned seventeen the month before, and here I was—a mama. I had postpartum blues so I cried every day for about two weeks, but I recovered. I guess every mother thinks this, but I *know* it—she was the most beautiful, perfect, little girl I had ever seen. I made her a promise that day to do my best by her. She is still beautiful and still perfect, and I am blessed by her every day. I have been honored and privileged to watch her grow up.

Stress

Then we decided to buy a bigger trailer. I remember our little girl was about two years old, and I was afraid for us 'cause we had lots o' trouble with our furnace in that trailer. It ran on kerosene, and I never knew when it was gonna catch fire. I remember one time somebody made a mistake and put fuel oil in the furnace. Oh—talkin' about fuel, that reminds me—that was another thing we had a hard time with, gettin' money for fuel. Anyway, this furnace, it was so old that sometimes it would flood with fuel and get too much of a blaze of fire in it. Real quick, of course, we'd have to disconnect the fuel line and let the flames die down. It was real scary. The water pipes were always freezin', too. I'd be worryin' since my husband would take a whole length of frozen pipe from under the trailer, bring it in the house, and thaw each one with kerosene heaters. It was bad and dangerous, and the trailer always stunk to high heaven like kerosene—leavin' me to wonder if those fumes were hurtin' our bodies. But what could we do? We survived that trailer time; it was our first little home, and it was *ours*!

There was lots of stressful times when my precious little girl was real young. The problem was that this one time, we decided to go into bigger debt and buy a bigger trailer. Terry, he came home this day (Kristina was only five weeks old) from the furniture factory where he worked, and he had a plan. I remember it clear as day—it was at his nine o' clock break from the mornin' shift that he came home sayin, "If you want a job, you be ready at noon, and I'll come pick you up." So it started: he came to pick me up, and we dropped off my little girl at his aunt's house. I really didn't like it, but I went along with the plan. I was breast-feedin', and I didn't know how to prepare for that. My breast leaked all day, and my shirt was drippin' and soppin' wet with milk all day, and my heart, it was totally broke. Also, to make things worse, my breasts felt like they would burst and I got what they called milk fever and I felt awful. I've heard somebody describin' leavin' a baby to go back to work when they're really small like "surgery without anesthesia," and I believe it—it was awful.

Anyway, we just kept workin' and workin', and my husband was so athletic and strong. I often said for the first eight to ten years of our marriage, "I'm married, but *he* ain't!" He played every sport there was, and he was really good at softball, so people would beg him to be on their teams. He'd join three teams at once and practice with all o' them during the week, so—go figger—that's one day per week with each team. Plus, he never missed them games. Bowlin' was another hobby he had; he even had a bowlin'-at-midnight team. He was good and he was competitive, so he was never home; I used to say he just came home to change clothes. We rode to work and from work together, and I used that time to beg him, "Why don't you spend time with me?"

God blessed me with a job in the final inspection department at Craftmaster Furniture Co. The workers called me and the other girls in our department the "Blow off Girls" cause we'd come to clean up the furniture with an airhose right before it went to the shipping department. Our equipment had lots of air pressure to blast the dust and debris off each piece of furniture. You'd never believe how dirty furniture can get during the building process. After blowin off the dirt we had to bend over and inspect each and every inch of every chair for random strings separating from the main fabric. Certain kinds of cloth was woven so lose that it could take thirty minutes to remove all the threads, especially when they'd frayed making the job almost impossible. Sometimes there'd be ten or twelve upholstering lines running at the same time; each line produced a lot of furniture. So we'd always be workin as hard and fast as possible. My position was one of the hardest and lowest paying jobs in the entire factory, but I knew I had to start somewhere.

All it seemed like I did was cook and clean, and he just did what he wanted. It was a long time before we even had a phone. I don't know what possessed me since we wasn't gettin' along, but somehow I decided to get pregnant. See, I knew I wanted two kids, so I figgered it'd be a good idea to just get it out o' the way. We couldn't afford it, but I got pregnant again anyway; no, I wasn't thinkin' clearly, and I got pregnant pretty quick.

God Throws Us a Rope

When I was pregnant with my son Johnathan and still workin', we was workin' really hard. Terry and I decided that since this was the last child we was gonna have, I was gonna stay home for six months. I remembered how hard it was to leave Kristina. The plan started out that I was to stay home for near a year and no less than six months, meanin' we would just have to live as frugal as possible. Bein' home, bringin' home no income was worth it so I could stay home with my children. Havin' other people takin' care of Kristina had made me so sad—I wanted to be the one home with with my own children.

Johnathan—July 2, 1987

Johnathan Andrew Bell
the happiest baby

With my precious son, I had a pretty smooth pregnancy. I worked full-time in the factory until four days before his birth. I remember I had a job that required me to be on my feet ten hours a day. I was so tired—I think there was times I almost fell asleep standin' up. On most days, I would get home and have to go to bed. Kristina was two and a half years old, and she needed me. I was filled with guilt 'cause I was so tired all the time. My sister Missy was livin' with us at the time, so she helped us so much.

We got off work June 28 for our July Fourth vacation, and Johnathan was born July 2. The doctor wanted to keep us an extra day at the hospital, but I left—I was so eager to get home to my little girl. I fell in love with my son the first day I knew he was there; it was so amazing.! He, too, was absolutely beautiful and perfect—and he still is! It has been such a joy to watch him grow into the wonderful person he is.

Havin' two healthy children, I knew God was blessin' me. He had give me first a girl, Kristina, and then a boy, Jonathan. These two children were the most beautiful children I'd ever seen in my life, and I was determined to provide them with a good home and a good life; I tried every day to do my best for both of them.

God Drew Us Near

While I was pregnant, my husband got a new job at Alexvale Furniture where he was upholstering, but not on a line like before. We were blessed 'cause this was a better job for better pay. Plus he was workin' with a good Christian man, Glen Joins, who became a special friend, coworker, and encourager to both Terry and I. Terry worked forty hours a week, and every day Glen would tell my husband, "It's your place to get your family in church." I think Glen knew that even though Terry and I was both saved at the age of twelve, neither him nor I had been grounded in church. We were both grateful to have been saved 'cause of church bus ministries, but we didn't get much church attendin' in our lives. I tell Glenn that I think he bugged Terry into submittin' and finally sayin' we would start goin' to church, or at least we would try it sometime.

So, when Jonathan was one week old, we went to church where Glen and his wife, Ann, went; they both had invited us, and when we got there all the people in that church, they just wrapped their arms around us, grabbed us, and loved us into that church. That's what Glen's and Ann's church did for us. I was kinda embarrassed 'cause I didn't even have clothes like the dresses and skirts all the other women wore. I had two skirts, a couple shirts, and I'd wear the same ones over and over; so people gave me personal clothes plus baby clothes for our children. They were all so kind, and I'll never forget Beulah's Baptist Church of Taylorsville, North Carolina. Thank all of you with all my heart!

I remember one night there was a revival right after we started goin' to church, and at that service Terry and I decided to rededicate our lives. There was a preacher named James Lockee, who preached a message on the little boy with the fishes, and I knew right then when I was standin' there in that pew durin' the invitation that just like the boy, I didn't have much to give. Regardless, I made my way up to the altar and rededicated my life. I said, "Lord, I don't have much to offer, but if you want it, here it is." Terry was with me, and we both gave our lives completely to the Lord at age twenty and twenty-two.

From that point on, we just did our best, and we had a lot to learn as far as the Christian life and what God expected. 'Cause we didn't have formal trainin', we latched onto what new teachin' we got, and we just took it one day at a time. Terry still did lots o' sports and stuff; it wasn't a magic new time by any stretch. Bein' saved and rededicated didn't change our lives completely or all at once, but we were growin' some and goin' to church. I started readin' Christian literature, anything I could get my hands on.

I went back to work when Johnathan was six months old and the bills had started pilin' up. I wanted to stay out till he was a year old, but that didn't work, so Terry got me a job at Alexvale Furniture doing another entry level job with really low pay, but I was thankful for it. Anyway, I worked there for a long time, about three years. One blessin' was that at work we was allowed to use headphones so

I could listen to Christian radio programs, with speakers like James Dobson and Elizabeth Elliott. Those people touched my life—I'd give anything to meet them and thank them!

A time came when all I listened to was Christian radio, TV, and church messages; Terry and I were both growin' in the Lord, but we didn't grow fast. We still had lots o' problems. I felt so neglected; my husband was still into all kinds of sports and time away, but we was okay. We was makin' it as a family, and I'm so thankful even though those years was hard. I was thankin' God every day that we had a family, a good place to sleep, plenty o' food to eat, clothes to wear, and, well, it was kinda like we was all a team. Even if my husband was gone a lot, he always cared about us, and he was nothin' like my daddy. I thank God for that and His presence in our lives.

We worked and grew together as a family

A Total Horrible Day

Like I was sayin', I'll always be grateful for God's presence and how He carried me through some purty awful times. Several of them I call the worst, most terrible days of my life. One such day happened to my whole big family. I was married and had two kids. Jonathan was about nine months old, and I was twenty. We lived in North Carolina, and at the time I had two sisters who lived in Virginia. We decided to take the whole clan to visit my sisters at Easter. Me and Terry and our children and some of my siblin's all went one Friday morning. My sister Mae was drivin' her boyfriend and her two children, my mama, my daddy, and two of my brothers; that was eight people in a little car. They were supposed to arrive Friday evening right behind us.

It got late and they didn't show. None of us had cell phones; actually most of us didn't have house phones neither. My uncle who lived in between North Carolina and Virginia called my sister's house about one in the morning and said someone told him that a Coleman family was in an accident, a bad wreck, and someone needed to come identify people. My uncle went and found my mama and a couple others there at the local hospital, but most everyone else had been airlifted to care in bigger cities.

Everyone was injured real bad 'cept Daddy and my sister's boyfriend. Uncle Charlie said the only way he identified my mama was by her feet—that her face was unrecognizable. The three worst victims were at Bristol Memorial in Tennessee. My brother James, who was seventeen, had a crushed hip and major head injuries. Mama was unconscious for two weeks, and my three-year-old nephew had a broken arm and other injuries. When I got to the hospital and saw these three loved ones in such bad shape, I was afraid to leave them. I stayed in that place with them for two full weeks. My sister Missy, who has always been my right hand, she took care of my children. That was our Easter vacation, and I'll never forget it.

Everybody recovered, but my brother James is forty years old now and has had three hip replacements, and he knows someday he may not be able to walk at all. All this is because of drugs and alcohol mixed with drivin'; my sister was the driver of that car, and she made some bad choices. The result was that James came home to live with me and still has hip and back problems today. Even though my sister had two children in two separate hospitals after the wreck—well, she still drinks alcohol today, and it makes me sad. As for me, I have no tolerance for alcohol or drugs—they have simply cost me too much and created in me too much pain. I don't want anyone I love takin' a chance with these substances. If this awful story keeps one person from drugs and alcohol—'specially from drinkin' or druggin' and drivin'—I'm glad I told it. I love my sister, and I know if she's got problems from the past that are affectin' her future, God is willing and able to help her. It's never too late.

"I Want My Daddy."

Another bad time was the day when I came home from work early, and there was no one home in our little bitty trailer. 'Fore I could put my pocketbook down, I got a call from Terry's sister. She said, "I have some bad news."

"Well, what is it?" I could barely speak 'cause my heart started poundin'.

"Well, he, your daddy, he was airlifted to Winston Salem—he shot hisself in the head."

I thanked her for callin' and lettin' me know. I put the phone down feelin' kind o' numb, and then I started screamin', "I want my daddy, I want my daddy," and I felt kind o' weak. He wasn't a good daddy, so I don't know why I had this reaction of havin' a hysterical fit, but I thought I'd pass out. A knock came at the door, and I remember it just happened to be my preacher and a couple from the church. Sobbin' and cryin', all I could mumble was, "My daddy, my daddy." I said, "I gotta go and see about my mama." My preacher told me he knew and he was ready and gonna take me up there. So we went to where my mama and daddy lived. Pullin' up to the house, we could see Mama—she was sittin' outside the house, which was taped off with bright yellow police tape. They wouldn't let her in; she was all covered with blood, and she was so drunk. Since they had airlifted my daddy to Winston Salem, I just took my mama home with me.

At that time, Terry showed up and helped me get mama home. I cleaned her up, and everybody in the family got dressed and we went to Winston Salem to the hospital. I called all my sisters and brothers up, and we met in Winston Salem at the Baptist Hospital and gathered 'round my daddy's bed. You could hardly recognize him. His head wasn't messed up 'cause o' the gunshot. That caused just a little tiny hole where the bullet went in and a little tiny hole where the bullet went out. They had him all wrapped up in gauze, and that wasn't what made him unrecognizable either. The swellin' up all over his body was what made him not look like hisself. I think that the part of the brain that controls temperature and all that stuff was all damaged. Anyway, we was all gathered 'round his bed, all us children, and I think the nurses had a hard time believin' that there was so many of us.

My mama didn't want to leave his side 'cause she felt bad for him, but she couldn't see good so I stayed with her and him. Some of my sisters and brothers stayed, but some went home; for three days, we stayed at the hospital cryin' out to the Lord 'round his bed. I kept prayin' 'cause I knew with all my heart that God was able and, if this was part of His plan, He would touch my daddy, cause him to wake up, and help him to give up alcohol. I knew Daddy would have to dry out 'cause he wouldn't be able to give up booze on his own. But I was thinkin' ahead. I started plannin' and hopin' that he wouldn't be able to go anywhere and get liquor on his own and that would help—and then we'd all live happily ever after. I remember cryin' out so many times sayin, "I want my daddy here," even though I was grown and I had two kids. But, anyway, it didn't happen.

We went home to take showers and change clothes 'cause it was only like an hour from the hospital to home. When we got there, they had already called people there to tell us that he had died. I felt like we let him down a little bit 'cause we wasn't present when he passed, but I don't think he was present in that hospital anyway. I was real mad at God for a while after this. I'd go to church, but I was only sittin' in the pew bein' angry 'cause God didn't save and fix my daddy.

I Couldn't Hardly Take It.

After that my mama came to live with us. At first—I'll have to be honest with you here—it was hard 'cause I was tryin' to make a new Christian home for my family and my children. She followed me 'round constantly; I didn't have no privacy. If anyone called, she wanted to know who it was, what did they want, what did they say, and so on. "Blah, blah, blah," is what I heard. That wasn't all. I think I had a lot o' resentment from past stuff, and I just started feelin' angry and frustrated. To make things worse, Mama would go spend the weekends with my sister Mae, and they would get real drunk and stuff and party at her house. Then Mama would come back all drunk, all dirty, and bruised up—like she'd wallered in the mud. Oftentimes she had peed on herself, and sometimes she could hardly walk. Anyway, I couldn't hardly take it!

Sometimes she'd bring beer and hide it in my house, and that's somethin' I would totally not allow. Well, we kept goin' to church and prayin' for her all the time, and I finally told Mama, "You have to make a choice: if you want to live with Mae, then go live with Mae, but if you want to live with me, live with me. Know you can't keep doin' this on weekends and then come here." That weekend, we was goin' to church, and Mama went along. I wasn't 'spectin it, but my mama, well, she got saved 'cause she asked Jesus to be her savior!

That Sunday was the start of a miraculous change in this woman. I'd heard about miracles changin' people, but I couldn't believe it. Before she got saved, she couldn't say a kind word about anybody; every other word was a cuss word, and she just looked and acted really mean and hateful. And after she got saved, she always acted like—well, just looked and acted like she felt gratitude, and that's what filled my mama for everything and everybody. She didn't say mean things about anybody no more, and she also never went back to my sister's no more. To this day, I know God blessed my mom 'cause He led me to set limits—she was changed 'cause, in my mind, God blesses boundaries. In fact, he blessed Terry, me and the kids with more worry free time to do fun things. I kept thinkin' *I could get used to this!*

My Sweet Mama
after she got saved, she wasn't mean anymore

We assumed the loan and moved into the house my mama and daddy had 'cause it was bein' foreclosed. We did a lot o' work on it, and we made it into a home big enough for everyone: Terry, my two children, my mama, my youngest sister and her daughter, and my brother Ray. Anyway, we had enough room, and my brother James assumed the loan on the trailer we'd been buyin'. We was glad he stayed there, and all the money we had paid on that trailer wasn't totally wasted. So, we had a pretty good life goin'. Every time the doors opened at Concord Baptist Church, we'd be there. I have to say at this point Terry and I had a lot o' growin' up to do, but we did our best to hold the family together. Still, bein' young, we both made a lot o' mistakes, meanin' we had to learn how to forgive and love each other through it all. God blessed us for hangin' tight, and we made it through.

You Want to Be a What?

My kids was nine and twelve maybe; I'm guessing at these ages, but it's pretty close. One day Terry told me he felt like he was called to preach. Well, I had seen enough to know that preachers' wives and children had extra pressure on them, and preachers do, too. So, I said, "It's hard enough to be a deacon's wife or a Sunday schoolteacher's wife—and here you want to be a preacher?" I plainly told him if I had wanted to marry a preacher, I would have married a preacher. I even said mean things like, "What makes you think you're good enough to be a preacher?" He always gave me the right answers, like when he said, "I'm not good enough, but He asked me to do it and I have to do it!"

Well, I tell you, it was about six months to a year's time that I warned him like every Sunday or every Wednesday—anytime at church when I sensed he was filled with conviction that he should become a minister 'cause o' what God was "tellin'" him to do. He'd be holdin' onto the pew with tears rollin' down his face at the altar call, and I'd say, "Don't do it! If you do it, you do it by yourself 'cause me and the kids, we ain't followin' you into this!" I just knew it would be too hard. I was so afraid for the stress and stuff it'd bring on our marriage and family.

Well, one Sunday, we was standin' in church, and he looked over at me and he said, "I have to answer to God for what I do, so I'm gonna do what He's asked me to do." So he told the church that he was called to preach, and, well, you talk about cryin'; tears rolled down my cheeks, and people thought I was happy and touched happy-like by all this. But no, I was not. See, I had gave him an ultimatum, and he had not chosen me; so to be honest, I didn't talk to him for three days. He begged and pleaded and bought me jewelry and stuff, and finally I said, "Okay, I'll go once in a while with you to do some preachin', but I want to be a part of my own church, too, 'cause I need that stability." You know what, every time he went, I went. We was in a different church constantly 'cause people was asking him to preach revivals and fill in on Sundays, and he was so capable and articulate—it was just purty amazin'!

God Don't Call the Equipped—He Equips the Called

Terry was a smart man, and God had His hands on him. I used to wonder, *how can any woman listen to her husband preach knowin' how ornery he might be at home?* But I tell you, when Terry preached, I actually was able to forget who was doin' the talkin', and all I heard was the message. I tell you, it was like Terry just disappeared and God did the teachin'—it was wonderful how God used that man. We traveled with him a lot. My daughter could play the piano and we would all sing, so we kind o' felt like a team. We had a pretty good life for about two years. I just knew that sometime Terry would get a church of his own 'cause he was in bible college studyin' close to home at the time and it sure seemed God was goin' to use him.

About this time, for a couple o' years, Terry had started dating me again, and—wow! Our relationship was wonderful. He would come to my work on Friday 'cause he got off early, and he'd bring my lunch and he'd bring me gifts. He started like courtin' me, and we had a good thing goin'. I couldn't hardly believe this was my life. We decided we'd do some paintin' on our house. So, we had everything moved out of our bedroom, and Terry was patchin' all the holes in the walls. Only thing we had in our room was a mattress in the room's middle on the floor.

There come a time I noticed that Terry started gettin' sleepy earlier and he'd been complainin'. Well, let me back up. For a month before, he'd been tellin' me about these super-bad headaches, so I made him an appointment at the doctor's. I was convinced it was his cholesterol or high blood pressure 'cause he'd put so much salt on his food, it'd be white. The doctor did a physical, and nothing was wrong. So I said, "Okay, it's your eyes." Well, we had that checked out, and they said his eyes was perfect. So I said, "Okay, it must be sinuses." I knew when I had sinus trouble, I had to take sinus medicine every day, so that must be what he had. So, now, every mornin', he'd get up with his headaches; it would hurt so bad that he'd be throwin' up. I was so afraid we'd lose our home or the stuff that we had worked hard for. I'd say stuff like, "World don't stop 'cause we got headaches," and "We have to keep goin'." I feel so sorry for that now. He'd get up, throw up from the pain in his head, and then he'd keep goin'.

Surely This Is Nothin'

Then one night we had the mattress on the floor, and Terry went to bed real early. I told him, "You're just startin' to get like me"—'cause lots o' times, I needed more sleep than he did. We wanted to stay up late that night, but we were both exhausted and we went to bed really early. Well, about three o'clock in the morning, Terry had a grand mal seizure, and I know now what I should have done: call 911. But I didn't call anyone. See, I had a sister who had epilepsy, and I thought the proper thing was always to just roll them on their side and let it pass. I'd seen a lot o' seizures, and I thought I could handle it. Plus I didn't want the ambulance to scare my mama and kids. I remember thinkin' that soon as daylight comes, we'd go to the doctor and figger out what's goin' on; he'd be on epilepsy meds, and we'd all be okay.

Well, that morning I got up and, truly, I never missed work, always wantin' to be counted present 'cause I didn't want it on my record that I laid off work even one day. So I planned the timin' really close. I was goin' to work like an hour, and then I'd come back home and take Terry to the doctor. I told Terry to be ready when I come back to take him to the doctor. He asked, "What for?"

"You had a seizure," I explained.

He argued with me, and he didn't believe me. I called one of his best friends, Glen Joines, and said, "Glen, knowin' you're off from work today, would you mind takin' Terry to the doctor 'cause he had a bad seizure last night? Could you take him to the urgent care center where Ann (Glen's wife) works?" So Glen agreed to takin' Terry; you see, these two guys, they was real close. I remember thinkin' Terry might not remember bein' told he had a seizure and the doctors might not do the proper tests. So, I asked Glen to stop by my work and pick me up so I could go with them. I'll tell you about a mass I found on my body the day before—but that's a story for later.

Roller-Coaster Feelin's Without the Fun

So, they picked me up, and we went to Statesville. By the time we was all in the car, Terry had changed. He was listless, he couldn't focus, he was almost unconscious, and I could tell somethin' was really wrong. We took him into the clinic and put him in a chair 'cause he could hardly walk. They got him to an exam room, and the doctor noticed things I had not seen: his skin was covered with these tiny little red dots. When I told the doctor about the seizure, he explained that it must have been a really bad seizure such that the strainin' almost caused the blood to come through the skin, and that's what made the dots. Glen had to leave the room for some time when they took Terry to do a CAT scan; then they took him for another test, leavin' me waitin' in the room by myself. Finally, after what seemed like a whole day, the doctor came in and told me that Terry had a real big tumor on his brain.

I said, "No, this is not possible 'cause he's very healthy and he's strong."

The doctor said, "Mrs. Bell, I can show you the tumor; it's there, and you need to get a grip on yourself because I'm gonna have to tell Terry. Then he needs immediately to go see a neurosurgeon, and so you're gonna have to get him to a hospital tonight."

So then I was able to step away from the pain and shock of all this and think of my family. I started to realize I can't go home this evening; so I did what I always did when I had problems: I called my sister Missy. She agreed to take care of my family that evening; and I called my best friend, Brenda—she had been my rock for many years. I just wanted prayers. I told Brenda, "Terry has a tumor."

"Where is it?" she asked.

When I told her, "On his brain," I could immediately hear her gasp from the pain those words inflicted. I also called Terry's sister 'cause I knew his family would want to know. Glen said he'd take us to Winston Salem so we wouldn't have to go by ambulance. They gave Terry some meds by IV, and they released us to go. When we got there, the first doctor we talked to was Dr. Wilson. He was so kind and so gentle as he explained that there was a specialist who did surgery on the left side of the frontal lobe. He said the tumor was pretty big. He explained how many types of tumors there was and that some are not cancer. So I decided this would be one of those that you remove and forget about, and then you go on with the rest of your life. I even started tellin' myself, "Look what a testimony Terry will have!"

Miracle in the Midst

I need to tell some history 'bout things that happened to my daddy in the past—things that led up to a huge blessin' for me, Mama, and Terry right at the same time we was facin' our greatest needs with Terry gettin' so sick. See, when Daddy come out of the coal mines, I was only about twelve years old; this was before we moved to North Carolina. Daddy hired a lawyer 'cause he had the black lung disease and he had to have lots of medical tests and treatments done. All through my life growin' up, my daddy would get letters from this lawyer; sometimes he told us it would say, "You've won your case—you're gonna get lots of money." Then another letter would come pretty quick, and it'd say, "We're sorry, the mining company's appealed the decision. You don't get anything until the appeal's decided."

This went on and on for seventeen long years; Daddy would get all excited and say, "I'm gonna buy this, I'm gonna buy that." We knew over these years of ups and downs that if he did get some money, for sure he would throw it all away, like on women or booze. I'd say to him, "I'll believe it when I see the check." Like I said, this went on so long that I think God knew to keep Daddy from gettin' the money. I'm convinced he would have blown it all, every penny of it. So, 'cause of his suicide, God didn't allow him to ever waste any of that money.

One day, it was about April 2, 1998, I had come home from work, and my husband was wavin' around a check that came for my mama; it was a large sum of money. Terry asked, "Can we cash this?" I was always fearful and skeptical, so I fast said, "No! We'll have to pay it all back!" At this time, my mama had been livin' with us and had been there ever since daddy's death. Terry and I, we totally covered all the livin' expenses for Mama, several of her kids, and our family. It had been real hard and we woulda' loved some relief. Still, not trustin' the check, I called the lawyer to ask about it, and the assistant said that for sure, "It's good—you can cash it—and there's more comin'."

My mama gave each one of her children some money. 'Cause Terry had done raised some of her children and she'd been livin' with us so long, our finances was purty bad. We'd been strugglin' and barely payin' our bills month to month. Mama always felt bad 'bout the support we'd be givin' the family, so now she wanted to pay our house off. I couldn't believe it; we wasn't gonna have to make those big house payments no more. It was such a blessin'; even though we didn't owe very much in total, the monthly payments were sometimes hard to make. What a miracle of timin' to have a paid-for house the first week in April, since on April 15, Terry had the seizure. You see, nothin' catches God by surprise.

I believe in my heart that every time that case went to court, the judge didn't see the case right and let the company appeal for seventeen years; that's a long time for this to keep goin' on. Then, that day in April of '98, I believe a judge was sittin' with this case before him, and an angel or God's Holy Spirit said, "No more appeals." So our house got paid off about one week before Terry had the seizure, the one event that stopped him from ever workin' again. I remember that I walked around with the "paid in full" piece of paper in my pocket every day, takin' it everywhere all the time and

100

no one knew. I'd read it whenever I was by myself, and then I'd read it again, and again, over and over to God. I'd catch myself sayin' out loud what I was thinking, "What did you do, God? Why have you been so good to us?" I just couldn't believe it! I didn't know it was comin', but God did. Since Terry couldn't work and only got a little from Social Security, we couldn't have survived if I'd had to continue makin' a house payment. Even with the house paid off, I had to work two jobs just to survive, and I couldn't have done much more.

The important thing is that I think—no, I know: things like this happen in everybody's life, but sometimes they don't see the hand of God in it. I thank Him that He let me know, without a doubt, that this gift was from Him. Ain't that just like God? We just have to be watchin' to see blessin's and give Him all the credit and glory!

I still have that tattered *"Paid In Full"*!

Those words remind me of what

Jesus Christ did for us when He hung on that cross.

What a price He paid—and it's

paid in full!

No Time for a Breakdown

Thank God our finances had got better 'cause right in the middle of this time when we was waitin' to schedule Terry's surgery, I found a mass in my body. It was big as a golf ball. I was in such a hurry takin' care of everyone that I neglected it. Once I finally got to the doctor, he poked 'round and asked if it hurt, how long had it been there, and the such. I started gettin' concerned when they told me we needed more tests. I remember overhearin' the doctor schedulin' a "biopsy" and mentioning a "mass."

When I got home, the family asked, "What did they say?" And to be strong for them, I said, "It's nothin'." But I was scared. I had heard them say them words *mass* and *biopsy*. So I cried privately and started cleanin'. I tore through the closets, cabinets, and anything I could find to clean. So, on the day before appointments to set Terry's surgery date, I checked in for my biopsy. As I sat waitin' for them to come take me into the OR, I remember thinkin', "If we both have cancer, who's gonna take care of our family?" Talk about fear!

Thank goodness it was only a hernia and they repaired it 'cause I was needin' to be there for Terry's surgery soon. I left right after they had finished my surgery even though they told me to stay awhile.

They gave Terry steroids for the swellin' on the brain and said they'd call us at home with the surgery date. I waited for that call, and it was the next couple o' days during this time that Terry was not right; he was actin' like a small child who needed help with everything. So we went and met with the anesthesiologist and stuff, and then the next day we showed up for surgery. I have to say that our pastor took us for these visits, and he was so good and kind. The nurses' team took Terry away, and our kids and his sister were there. I was in a pretty good mood 'cause I refused to accept that this would be one of those bad tumors. Well, after the surgery, the doctor came out into the surgery waitin' room askin' for Mrs. Bell. He suggested we walk down the hall, and he told me they had a path report and the tumor was called a glioblastoma and was a grade four, meanin' the prognosis is bleak. The doctor said Terry had about nine months of quality life, at most, because there aren't too many treatments or much medicine can do.

I couldn't believe it! Once again, my world was crumblin' down around me. I wanted to curl up and die myself. But I didn't have time to collapse. I remember thinkin', "I'll have a nervous breakdown, but I don't have time." I just had to keep walkin' 'cause the doctor said we needed to go together to tell Terry. Well, I tried to be strong for him, but we went into the recovery room where he was, and seein' him with his head bandaged up was so hard. He was alert but couldn't talk; he knew everything that was goin' on. The doctor told him he had cancer and that the prognosis wasn't good.

The Plan: The Best Dang Nine Months Ever

The doctor told him it was cancer and there wasn't much he could do. Terry and I cried and cried; I stood all night over his bed and sobbed. The next morning, they moved us to a regular room, where we tried to talk and understand. We decided maybe the doctors was wrong. If not, then even if we did have only nine months, we'd make it the best dang nine months anyone had ever had! Well, he was walkin' the next day with big bandages on his head; he was doin' great. They was callin' him the "star patient." His hair was gone on one side of his head. A sweet nurse brought in a pair of clippers and cut the rest of his hair off, even though hair was the least of our concerns.

He did really good the first day we got home, but then he didn't sleep well 'cause in our bed his head couldn't be elevated. We decided we was goin' to go buy a recliner the next day; Terry started kiddin' me that he'd always wanted one anyway. We got to that furniture store real early so we'd be sittin' there waitin' when they opened up. I looked over at him and saw his face was swellin' real bad, so I said, "Terry, how are you feelin'?" He said, "Okay." I could still see his face swellin' right in front of me. I told him, "We're goin' home, not furniture shoppin'," and I called the nurse as soon as we got home, tellin' her about his swole up head. She said, "Oh, that's all normal." All that day, I called back and forth to the nurses until Terry started throwin' up. At one point, he said he was in such pain that the pain meds, they wasn't doin' nothin'. His sister called to check on him and said if I had to go back to the hospital to call her and she'd take us real quick. So, I called the nurse back one more time, 'cause at this point he'd got a high temperature. She said to bring him in immediately.

The Longest Day

His sister came, and we drove more than an hour to get there and Terry was moanin' he hurt so bad. He was in the backseat, wincin' with the pain; it was so hard to watch. When we got to the emergency room in Winston Salem, we saw there were lots of doctors in that place; it was a teachin' hospital. Believe me, I think everyone needs to learn on somebody, but I have to say I'll never let somebody learn how to stick a spinal tap on someone I love again. Terry was feelin' so bad, and the doctor in trainin' stuck him four times. He screamed out 'cause it was so painful. Well, they showed me what they got out in the syringe. The doctor said the fluid was supposed to be clear, but it was totally cloudy. He was guessin' there was a real good chance that Terry had meningitis. Then he said, "This is a serious condition, and it could be fatal."

I didn't know what they was doin'; they was hookin' him up to things fast, and they asked me to step out. So, I remember as plain as day, steppin' out into the hall and watchin' them take Terry straight to the ICU. All I kept hearin', over and over in my head, was, "It could be fatal." So there I stood in this busy emergency room hallway, knowin' medical people was workin' on my husband and he wasn't hardly conscious. I knelt down, layin' my head in my hands, leanin' on a buggy of dirty laundry, and I didn't think a bit about who was passin' me by. There were workers everywhere, busy rushin' around—I didn't care. I cried out loud, "God, I thought we was gonna get nine months. We want our nine months!" And with beggin' and remindin', I told Him, "I knelt in those wood shavin's and asked you to save me—now I'm yours, and I need your help."

ICU

The next days were spent in ICU. I was so mad, and I was just devastated. I kept thinkin' and tellin' the Lord, "I had plans, Lord—what about my plans?" After they got Terry settled in the unit, his sister made her phone calls to her family, and I made my calls to my family. When you are there with a patient in this kinda care for someone who could die, they take you to a waitin' room and they call you once an hour or so to go in and visit. When you go in, you know it might be the last time, so you sure don't want to leave and miss any o' those times. I went in every chance I got, and I stayed in the waitin' room constantly; they had a locker so I could keep stuff there. My sister Missy, I have to say, her and her husband they went right to my house, filled our spots, and took care of our family. It was a big family: we had my mama, my brother Ray, my sister, my niece, and my two children. But Missy didn't hesitate; she packed up their two kids and moved in and took care of things.

I didn't know how long I'd be there, but I stayed every day he was there. I remember sayin' to anyone who'd sit still to listen: "Nobody knows my Lord like I do. He didn't fix my daddy, but he's gonna come through for me now. Daddy wasn't any good; he wasn't worth his salt. My husband here, I need my husband, and my kids, they need their daddy." So I just knew God would come through for me. I told the doctors and nurses what a wonderful man he was, so they wouldn't just think of him as the guy in bed number 4. I wanted them to know I needed him so badly.

You Wanna Do What?

Terry stayed in ICU, and day by day he got worse and worse; the surgeon said they couldn't find an antibiotic to fight the bug that was growin'. They had like towels wrapped 'round his head, and his head was gettin' bigger and bigger. The towels would get soaked with this fluid; his brain had an abscess in it, so they took him to surgery to clean off his infected tissue every other day. They'd bring him back, and this went on in ICU for a week and a half.

Sometimes I had visitors. Terry's mother and his sister decided to come and sleep in the waiting room at the hospital with me sometimes and I really appreciated the company. One night when his mother was there, we was tryin to stay up, but it was so late and there weren't any more visits scheduled, so we fell asleep. All of a sudden, a really young doctor named Dr. White came in wakin me up and askin to speak to me. "I need permission to do a procedure that I think might save Terry's life. He's been getting worse and worse, having strokes, and I need to do a procedure, opening three drainage holes up in his head to relieve the pressure on his brain. If I don't do something, he is going to die," the doctor said. I had seen Terry earlier that day, and he was packed in ice 'cause his temp wasn't regulated. (That's the way my daddy was before he died.) So, I knew I better say to go ahead, and I gave him permission without knowing what else we could do.

So, next thing I knew, in the middle of the ICU, with no sterile environment, this doctor, he took a drill and drilled three holes in Terry's head. He inserted somethin' like straws into his head with no X-ray guidance. The tubes stayed in his head a couple o' weeks, and the medical team put antibiotics in them and suctioned out the excess fluid. A special group of infectious disease doctors showed up; they were all wearin' protective outfits—kinda like toxic-waste people. Amazin', but this team was tryin' to find an antibiotic to help. Well, it was amazin' what they brought; within a day, the medicine had started workin'. I felt like we had the best doctors possible 'cause they finally figgered out somethin' that worked. I believed that whole team came to save Terry's life, and that God Himself had sent them.

A Ray of Hope

Pretty soon he started gettin' better. After another two and a half weeks, he got a regular room, and they said soon he'd go to rehab. He'd had a stroke, so half of his body didn't work. I remember somethin' funny that happened. I didn't leave his room much since he didn't want to be alone 'cause he got frightened. One night I finally went down to the cafeteria, and rather than wake him, I looked at the lowered side of the bed where his weakness was, and I just left it down. I figured he was too paralyzed on that side so he couldn't move that direction. When I came back in the room, I saw the bed was empty and wondered where they took him. Then I heard his voice say, "I'm down here." I said, "What? Where are you?" Terry had fallen out of the bed and managed to crawl under the bed 'cause I guess he was scared. The nurses had to come put him back, and they had a good laugh with us. I kinda felt like it was my fault he fell, but the nurses was so kind. They said no one else in Terry's shape could've gotten out of bed, much less crawled under one.

Anyway, I stayed with Terry this whole time, and my kids came to visit and other people did, too. They told us we was going to the Stick Center, the rehab, and normally they didn't want anyone to spend the night with patients, 'cause they wanted them to work harder. I told the nurses I didn't want him to be sad, 'cause he just found out he had cancer and had only a few months to live; I didn't want him to be by hisself. So, I just stayed and tried to be a help to them, and I liked these people; they were so nice. Lots of friends and family came to visit Terry. It always lifted us up to have company. The day we got to go home was a wonderful day!

Lots o' hospital stayin' days, I thought about just goin' home. One day in particular, I was determined to leave with the kids since I had not been home in almost five weeks. My daughter was fifteen and my son was eleven, and these children were beggin' me to come home. My heart was broke 'cause I just knew my kids needed me. I packed up all my junk and told Terry, "Bye." He begged me to stay. I got to the elevator and had a change of heart. Cryin' like a baby, I told them, "If this was you, I couldn't leave you. You aren't the one that's sick, your daddy is, and I need to be here." They cried and cried so it was hard, but I went back and stayed with Terry.

A New Life

Finally Terry got to go home, and what a blessin' to sleep next to my husband, to cuddle up next to his big body. And somehow he and I, we began a lifestyle that was different. I had to go back to work as soon as possible. My brother Ray and my mama, they was legally blind and they couldn't see good. Then there was Terry—he couldn't get 'round good. Still, they all looked after each other. Terry couldn't drive for a long, long time, so we just began a lifestyle of stayin' home 'cept for doctor's appointments at times I could get off workin'. We just made it a life; it was different. But we was together, and we was okay.

Terry had therapy at home for a long time. A guy from church came and put a rail on our steps and to our bedroom. The brace Terry wore wasn't real comfortable. I had to keep tellin' him, "Pick your foot up, pick your foot up." He had one foot that never healed from them strokes, so it was always draggin'. It was hard for my kids to see their daddy havin' problems. I made a decision to always try to be honest with them 'bout the situation; I didn't want no surprises or to be hearin', "You lied—I thought you said everything was okay." So after we got home, I went in my little girl's room; she was fifteen at this time. I just told her we probably just had about nine months with her daddy, but that "We'll still be okay—we'll still be a family." I tried to reassure her that we'd make it somehow and that I was gonna take care o' them.

I did the same thing with my son, but he was just eleven and I just didn't know how to deliver it. What I did was I saw him ridin' his little bicycle up and down the road, so I went out and told him to come over to me 'cause I wanted to talk. He would ride his bicycle beside me as I walked and talked. He would bike a little next to me, then he'd leave, then he'd come back. It was like he had to go digest it. Anyway, I just told him how it was and it broke my heart to tell my kids these things, but I felt like it was important to tell it like it really was. I have to say they were brave and they was the best kids in the world, even though our life was kind of just wait and see.

Terry lived for five and a half years instead of just nine months. He taught me how to pay bills, balance the checkbook, go to the bank (those tubes suckin' up those cylinders—they plumb terrified me; I was so afraid I'd do it wrong or get hurt somehow), go grocery shoppin', and all kinds o' stuff. He'd managed all these things before 'cause he planned the budget and he was so smart with numbers and math. I'd be amazed he could tally up our bill just looking at our shoppin' basket. I relied on him for all these things, but he taught me pretty quick.

We went to lots of doctors' appointments. Sometimes we had good reports where they would look at his MRIs and there would be no more tumor, and sometimes there would be tumors. There was radiation for six weeks in a row—that was forty-two days in a row. I'd actually work till lunchtime, and then I'd go with him to his radiation treatment. I don't know why, but I wanted to be there for him 'cause these treatments were kind o' scary. They had created a mask of plastic mesh that fit over his face and head, and they bolted his head to like a board; it kept his head completely still. They explained that his head had to be still 'cause if he moved his head and the radiation got into his healthy brain tissue, it would destroy the healthy part of his brain instead o' the tumors. Anyways, every time he had radiation, this thing would be placed over his head and then he was bolted down; it was just plain terrifyin'. Durin' these treatments, the radiation therapist was wonderful, and the oncologist was wonderful. We could not have asked for better. I know we had the best doctors and medical people in the world.

But it was just constant medical appointments. We'd always be wonderin' what they'd find. Sometimes they'd see a tumor, sometimes not; it was very intense. Nine months passed, and he was doin' great and we was feelin' and tellin' people, "Thank you, Jesus." We was gettin' along pretty well. Terry was doin' more around the house 'cause I was workin' so much, and he was a good man. He was still goin' to school to the bible college, which he started before he got sick. He studied a lot, and he cooked and cleaned for a long time. In fact, actually some of my work friends were pretty jealous 'cause I'd go home to a warm, cooked meal. That was our lifestyle, but, due to all the surgeries and the tumors comin' back, well, Terry changed.

The doctor, he told me that your frontal lobe kind of inhibits your behavior and what you say. Well, for Terry, that was missin', so he would just kind o' blurt out whatever came to his mind. And so, even in public, if he saw a fat lady, he would say, "Hey, there's a fat lady," or whatever he'd be thinkin'. And he would do that with our kids. So, of course, he hurt lots o' feelings. I tried to explain it was 'cause he couldn't help it, but even at church he would say things. It was funny at times. One Sunday at church, he was called on to pray, and he said somethin' that was not appropriate and all the congregation near busted out laughin'. It just became part of our life, and our relationship changed; I ended up being the excuse maker and the caregiver. It felt like I had the weight of the world on my shoulders.

I have to say, at this point I know God was helpin' and God was providin'; He was blessin' us. But it still felt like a lot to carry, like I had this big family strapped on my back. It felt just real heavy— that's the only way I can describe it. There was a lot of worry and stress I was carryin' alone. Terry and me weren't like husband and wife; we was more just caregiver and sick one. Time was spent at lots of appointments, with me feelin' isolated and not understood.

Carryin' On Like Normal: Miss Priss

Even though I was feelin' discouraged, I tried to carry on with normal family life as much as I could. Bein' out doin' normal things gave me some days I could laugh at when they was over. One of these days was all about one of my pets. We had one little girl puppy we dubbed "Miss Priss," and she was my favorite. She was born with somethin' wrong with her throat, and this caused real bad breathin' problems. This condition grew worse with each passing day. Well, on the very day close to the time we needed to leave for the airport to pick up my daughter's boyfriend, our sweet Miss Priss started havin' the worst time ever—gaspin' for air. She even started havin' seizures from not gettin' enough oxygen to her brain.

I called the vet and he was closin' up his office so he was perturbed, but he agreed to put her down if we came right then.

It was on our way to the airport, and even though we was already runnin' behind, I insisted on goin' by the vet's office, despite the protests of my teenage daughter and my husband. We stopped, and the vet quickly did what had to be done. I was so sad when I walked out of the office with my little puppy's body; I wrapped Miss Priss in a towel like a baby and held her tight, just like a little baby.

The airport was an hour away, and we didn't have time to take the puppy back home. Since I figgered it would be the last time I would see her, I decided to just hold her in my arms for the whole trip. Now, I didn't know that her little body would start expelling bodily fluids, bodily waste, and some gasses that was so strong we was forced to roll the windows down. Still, I cradled the puppy in my arms with my husband gagging and my daughter whining about what her boyfriend would think. They both begged me to at least put her in the trunk. I refused 'cause I loved this little puppy.

We got to the airport to pick up Dennis, the boyfriend, and Kristina went in to find him; me and her dad and the puppy waited in the car. We waited for what seemed to be forever, so I decided to go look for my daughter. She was only seventeen, and I had a lot o' scary visions in my head. I put my little bundle (which probably looked like a baby 'cause of how I wrapped and carried it) in the trunk and went in to find my daughter.

This was right after 9/11, so the airport was swarmin' with soldiers with real big guns. My husband began to drive around this little circle where you pick people up. Well, I don't know if they saw him make one too many trips around the circle or if they wanted to know about the bundle in the trunk, but when they asked him to pull his car to the side, they questioned him a little. He had a hard time answerin' since several brain surgeries and radiation had taken a toll on his being able to find the right words.

When we got to the car, the police had the car surrounded, and they was tryin' to get him to explain why he had a dead dog in his trunk drivin' circles 'round the airport. I think they thought he was a terrorist or somethin'. Anyway, I explained the whole thing. They bought it, I guess, 'cause they let us go. So you can 'magine my husband was furious and my daughter embarrassed, but my little Miss Priss got to go home and have a proper burial.

Attendin' Meetin's

I'll never forget the time I talked myself into goin' to a support group meetin' someone told me about. A friend said I had to go to get some encouragement. So, tired as I was, I went on to the meetin', not knowin' anyone there. Still, I was hopin' and thinkin' the people would understand just how I felt, and maybe they could tell me how I could feel better. In fact, I remember this was the group called "Brain Tumor Grief Support," and, well, I sure knew about grief. The problem was that after I sat there listenin' for what seemed like forever, I could see it was endin' up bein' support for how to cope *after* the death of a loved one who'd already died from a terminal brain tumor. I sat bein' quiet and respectful through the whole talk, but after they finished, I looked at those young girls who was leadin' this meetin'. I was determined to get one off to the side. I did just that, and I asked, "What about me? He's not died, but I lost him already." I just cried and cried and asked, "What do I do about the grief that I have to deal with now?" These girls was nice, but didn't have much to offer me. I know they was tryin to help but there just weren't many people who could identify with my situation.

The Pit

I felt so sad. My life just felt miserable, and I saw no end in sight. I kind o' felt like I didn't have a husband or a partner, and I felt like I had a whole lot o' people dependin' on me. I don't know exactly when, but I went to a doctor and I got on some medication, which made me kind of embarrassed. Plus, I started seein' a Christian counselor. I'm grateful I could stop leanin' on my friends so much, but things just didn't look good and my outlook on life was gloomy. It was like I couldn't believe that every time I turned around, things kept gettin' worse and worse.

Terry's condition was gettin' more bad as far as him bein' mobile and the way he acted. Over the two to three years into it, he got real mean. I'm sure he got angry 'cause he couldn't drive. He kind o' blamed me for a lot of stuff. I'd be tired from workin', and I would come home and I just wanted to rest.

I had a hard job workin' on a production line in a furniture factory, which meant I got paid accordin' to how much I did. That kind of pressure just felt like I could never do enough. Production work was like this: I'd get to where I was good at it and I'd start to make a little bit more money, and then the owners, who set them rates of pay, they'd see us close to makin' more and they'd change the rates. So, I'd be workin' more and more and makin' less and less. There was no legal contract to protect me or any of the workers. All this made me feel like I was bringin' home an empty cup again. I could *never* do enough, and I did it for ten years. Still, I was thankful for a job. It was so hard constantly feelin' like I was comin' up short. Incentive pay is a cruel thing to do to people!

So, in a typical day, I'd come home from work feelin' worthless at my job, and I just wanted to hide from the stress. Standin' at the door, there'd be my mama with her pocketbook on her shoulder and Terry would be waitin' on the couch, 'cause neither could go anywhere without me. Sometimes I felt bad, but sometimes I'd just say, "No, I'm not goin' nowhere." This would disappoint them and make them mad. Other times I'd give in, and sometimes resent it. Life was so hard.

I had a teenage daughter, and, well, that has its own stresses; she was a good girl, but you know she was makin' some choices that were makin' me afraid. I'd be worryin', too, 'bout my son; he was just bein' neglected. Anyway, my life just spiraled downward, and I felt like there was no end. About five years into all this, I remember just bein' so unhappy with my life. It didn't help much that Terry and I were not gettin' along good. We had no kind of relationship 'cept that I was his boss. I'd say, "Have you taken your medicine?" He was in charge of his own meds, and sometimes he'd get mad and just wouldn't take them. I hated my life and I hated the way me and him fought all the time 'cause I was the enforcer of what the doctors said he had to do. I remember sittin' outside of a doctor's office and it was Christmas at the five-year mark, and I was so sad. My friend Barbara was there, and all I could do was cry. I was realizin' that people got sick of my cryin', but I couldn't help it. I kept tellin' my friend Barbara that I didn't think I could take it no more.

So I told my preacher, "If Terry gets a good report, meanin' if there's no new tumors then I'm gonna take him to his mama's and let him stay there for a while. But if there is new disease," I explained, "I'll take care of him 'cause I know it's my duty and 'cause I told Terry I would be there." I made that commitment, but I kept thinkin' if only he was well enough, then I needed a break. Anyway, they did a biopsy on a little place, and it was more tumor. So, next there was many tests to see how aggressive it was. Again, we heard not good news; it was very aggressive cancer. The poor man, he tried to carry on and keep goin' to school, but he was just not hisself. This tumor was growin' at a rapid pace and he was havin' more seizures each day, and this was in December 2002.

Can't Take Much More

Then, five months later, in May, my mama got real sick. She'd been sick before and been through a lot, but this time she got so sick she couldn't hold her head up. I'd been takin' her to the doctor like once a week, and finally at one visit, they did a chest X-ray and told us it was all clear. Then a month later at the hospital, they come and told me she had lung cancer, and that she was eat up with it all over her heart and lungs and there was nothin' they could do. I said, "How's this possible when a month ago she had a chest X-ray and you all didn't see anything?" The doctor said sometimes it just don't show up. Well, he promised to make arrangements for hospice to bring a bed and help me. I couldn't believe it—my husband was gettin' worse, plus he was meaner and meaner and more and more helpless, and now here my mama was gettin' sick and gonna die. The doctor said she had only six weeks at the most.

Well, the thought of losin' my little mama at that time was so hard. I was workin' two jobs, so from the hospital I made the call to the restaurant, and I told them I wouldn't be back 'cause I had to take care of my mama. Next, I called my brother James and asked him to make a place for this hospital bed to be set, and he did. He fixed it perfect just from our conversation, and he fixed the room just like I wanted it. What a support team I had: my siblin's, my church, and my community—they all helped me so much. Well, my little mama came home from the hospital and the bed was waitin' for her, but I never told her why. See, this twelve years my mama lived with me, she kinda became, well, our relationship became like she was my child and not my mama. She clinged to me to be sure everything was okay. I don't mean this to be disrespectful, but my mama, well, she wasn't like most people's mamas. She wasn't quite right in the head, never. Now she was becomin' even more childlike; that's what she was, a child.

I just didn't tell her about her sickness, and I asked the doctor not to tell her 'cause I knew she'd spend the rest of her days frightened and cryin' and unhappy; the doctor agreed. So when I brought her home, I just told her she needed to stay in the hospital bed 'cause that'd be easier to help her get better. I told her the goal was to get her well so she could stay home instead of goin' to the hospital since she was very afraid of hospitals. I asked everybody who come by to not say anything. I hope I did the right thing, but I never told her that she was gonna die. Maybe she knew; I'm not sure. I still had to work my regular job. My sister Mae, she'd come take care o' Mama during the day, and I'd take care of her at night. My brother Ray, he helped a lot if we needed somethin' like liftin' or movin' stuff. He couldn't see good, but he helped with physical stuff 'cause he was strong.

Durin' my mama's sickness and stayin' in that hospital bed, Terry was just runnin' 'round sort of like a toddler, and he developed a problem and couldn't control his pee. So he'd be peein' everywhere, and he started havin' to wear these undergarments. I tried to keep that from his kids 'cause I didn't want them to see how bad it was gettin'. One day, he was actin' kind o' funny, and I remember he ran down the hall. Well, really he was not runnin', but kind of slidin', 'cause of his weak leg. Anyway, he started scootin' out in the hall in his underwear, causin Jonathan to ask, "Why does Dad have a big pull-up on?"

I kept tryin' to take care of my mama, and lots o' days there'd be lots o' people visitin': a nursin' team, a church team, and random church people. Our house was, I heard it described, like a hotel lobby. The doctors said they gave Mama six weeks, and she ended up with only five weeks. Durin' her sickness, it did not seem like she was in bad pain, thank God. She was as happy as she always was; she got real, real skinny and had bedsores, but she seemed okay. Sometimes she would have these respiratory attacks where she couldn't breathe and she'd be gaspin' for air. She'd cry out to the Lord to take her home. Again, thank God, these times, they weren't that often. I'd have to call the nurse and ask them for help in the middle of the night, and then I still had to go to work the next day. It was a competitive workplace, and I had to keep that job; it was the future for me and my kids.

all my siblings together three days before mama died

I remember purty clear the last hours of Mama's life. She was kinda unconscious and not too aware; all her children were 'round her bed. We was singin' her favorite hymns, and we saw an amazin' sight. Her eyes opened and she looked upward, and a smile appeared on her tired, thin face. She kept this peaceful face until the end, and we are all convinced she saw wonderful things we were not able to see. And so, my little mama died, and it was sad. Odd thing is that the truth is, I felt a little of the weight lifted from me 'cause I was no longer responsible for Mama. I missed her, but then real quick I started feelin' relief, which made me feel guilty, and 'bout then, I felt good from the relief, and so it went. Talk about a hard time!

The blessin' is that in the end, God had gave us back our mama, even though the devil tried to destroy her for some time. We never doubt now where she is, and I look forward to the day when I can tell her again how much I love her.

The Last Days

When my mama died, it was about that time Terry was hospitalized again. He'd had so many seizures that he'd lost the ability to talk. When I brought him home from the hospital this last time, he was real sweet and lovin'. Right before my mama passed, the doctor had recommended I get hospice for Terry, so I already had two hospital beds in my house. I had to have help 'cause Terry was peein' everywhere. The hospital bed helped, but I couldn't always get those undergarments on him. Sometimes it was just easier to change his sheets. Thank God, Terry was still mobile and in a real sweet stage, like a big, lovable toddler. He was on chemo at this time, and the doctor said it only had a 10 percent chance of workin', but I knew Terry would want to try for that.

While he was takin' chemo, I took twelve weeks off from my job at Broyhill Furniture so that I could stay home. It was allowed 'cause of the Family Leave Act; it was an unpaid leave and I really couldn't afford it, but it was what we both needed. I am so glad I had that time with him 'cause I needed a little bit of rest and I needed to be with Terry while he was still around. I felt like I had neglected him all these years. He got less and less mobile and couldn't communicate; he spiraled down during these twelve weeks, and he couldn't get out of bed without assistance. Gettin' worse each day, he needed constant care and couldn't do anything for hisself. He even needed to be propped up in a chair 'cause he'd fall over since he was so weak. I couldn't believe my big, strong man was gone, and in his place was this helpless child.

It was so hard to go back to work, but my time off was up and I had to. I knew my sister Mae, who took care of Mama, would agree to stay with Terry during the day, and then I'd give her my van as my payment. Well, I was back at work at my job for two weeks, and I remember Terry was still gettin' worse. I went to work one day and got a call from home from the hospice lady. She said, "Karen, call your kids and come home." My daughter was at college, and John was thirty minutes away. That day Terry had that rattlin' noise in his chest and he had "that face." Anybody that deals with death knows there's a face that comes to a person who's goin' to die. Their mouth makes a circle, and they don't look like the same person. It ain't that you look like yourself and you die; it's almost like you see a different person—it can even seem like a scary face of someone else.

My kids came and we held each other tight; all his family came, too. I told his sister and she notified all her family, so the house became swarming with people who loved Terry. So many came from everywhere. In a way, if I had it to do over again, it woulda been a private thing; I woulda just had it between me and the kids 'cause the way it was it became kinda crazy. It was way too crowded, too loud, and the hospice workers kept saying, "It will be anytime now." We was all smushed in my little home startin' at lunchtime that day, and I think he died at eight thirty in the evening. Part of the time, it felt like a crowded mall. Then there were special times, like when we stood 'round his bed and sang hymns. The hospice workers who worked the morning shift stayed the whole time, even though they had families of their own. I had good people around me; they felt kind of like angels. Without these people, I would not have made it.

Lessons from Terry

So, Terry passed away, and when he died, even more people came and were fillin' the house. I took my kids in my bedroom and I shut the door; I just held Kristina and Jonathan, and I kept sayin' I was so sorry. Also, I told them Terry died to show us how to die—how to do it right. He didn't die a bitter man, and he didn't question God's will. He was frightened and neither of us believed he would die, but Terry was real at times, too. He'd say, "I'm a winner either way" and "I'm trying not to ask why me, but why not me." I think Terry was here to be a blessin' to lots o' people, not just to take care o' me. He was a beautiful person. I'll always love him.

Numb

So, the next day I had to make arrangements. I wanted him to have a good funeral. For both him and for my mama, who had died three months earlier, I wanted a good send-off, and I felt like they both deserved it. So, I made sure both of them had good funerals. After that, I took another week off from work by tellin' my boss, "I just buried my husband, so I won't be there for a week." I sure needed a little time to clear my head, and that was my life.

Purty soon the hospital beds was all cleared out, and by this time in my house, it was only me and my brother and my son. I have to say that it was peaceful. I even had a dog that I had to put down two weeks after Terry died, and I remember comin' back from that ordeal and I felt relief. Then, like when Mama died, I felt guilty, startin' to argue with myself: this voice in my head was sayin', "Hey, this was your family, this was your pet, how can you feel relief?" Still, to be honest, I did feel a sense of bein' saved from stress, while at the same time I did stress 'cause I missed them so bad. Talk about a mix of emotions. I remember wonderin' what I was gonna do, what would my life be like.

My Prince

So many hard times happened to me growin' up and into adult life and all the way through to Terry's death. So now, I just have to bring you up-to-date with what's goin' on in my life now and how God has blessed me and made good things happen in my life. Not long after Terry died, this guy named Brad Gryder started to call, askin' if there was anything he could do. During one of these offers, I jokingly said, "Come take my trash off." Next thing I knew, there he was, helpin' my brother load my smelly trash in his truck. He never even stopped so I could thank him. He did call a few days later and asked if I wanted to go for a hike. Well, I knew his mom and that they was good people. I had seen Brad before with a group that ate at the restaurant where I worked in the past, and, to be honest, I was so lonely. I wanted someone to share things with, to listen to me, and to protect and be close to me; I needed to heal from the grievin' so bad. So I agreed to go somewhere, but I gave specific instructions that I would not be seen in town with a new man so soon after my husband's death. "What would people think, and what would the busybodies say?"

We started hangin' out, and Brad was the kindest, most compassionate man; he listened to me cry for my mom, who had died three months before, and he listened to me cry for Terry. I told him I didn't blame him if he ran away and never came back, but he stayed near. I am convinced my Heavenly Father knew I needed a comforter with skin on and He picked out Brad for the job. Brad was also a rare find because he was in his forties and had never been married and never fathered any children. We come from a small town, and to come upon a man with these qualities was rare indeed.

I told my kids about Brad right away. I didn't want to keep things from them 'cause I never had. My sweet Kristina, who was now a junior in college, was happy for me; but my Son, who was a junior in high school, had to think about it for a little. But soon Jonathan decided he wouldn't have to worry about me bein' so alone if I had a man friend. Well, like I said, Brad was there through the grievin' process and it wasn't purty. I was sad, I was angry, and I wanted my family back. I just couldn't understand why God would allow these things in my life. As I worked through these things, Brad was a shoulder to cry on and an ear to listen.

I couldn't believe it when I realized I was in love with Brad. The revelation happened when I went out to supper with another guy, who some of my girlfriends considered to be the "best catch" in Taylorsvillle. Bein' real smart, successful, never married before, and havin' no kids added up to a "desirable catch"; on this date, though, I was wishin' I was with Brad. I have to say, just because my heart had room for Brad doesn't mean I lost my love for Terry; somehow it remains. But I know in my heart that Terry did the work God had for him and then he got to go home. I still miss him and think of him every day. I feel bad for Kristina and Jonathan and their loss—especially at graduations and weddings.

Well, I had been datin' Brad for a year, and he finally asked me to marry him. I was speechless, but I could nod my head real big. I got married at the same church where we had the funerals for Mama and Terry. I had the weddin' I had always wanted. You know the kind: the long, white dress ($25 at a thrift store), flowers, candles, presents, and I even had a cake with the bride 'n' groom on top. Wow! I felt like Cinderella. My daughter was my maid of honor, and my son gave me away. What a happy day!

Me and Brad July 23, 2005
I felt blessed to find a handsome prince and to find a dress

Now it bothered some of the old busybodies in my town because I wore white, but I figgered I'd wear what I wanted 'cause I'd be payin' for it. When I came down that aisle, my heart almost exploded with joy; it was one of the happiest days in my life. By the way, there was standing room only—that's how good people was to me.

We was married for three months, and God opened my womb and I conceived. I couldn't wait to tell Brad, so I went lookin' and found him in the kitchen. He wrapped his arms 'round me and prayed a prayer of thanksgiving for this unbelievable blessin'. On August 8, 2006, we was blessed with our little Eva Grace; her middle name is for what God has done for her mama. She is smart and beautiful; we've wanted more children, but just haven't had any success. We would love to adopt maybe someday.

Eva Grace Gryder
Her biggest smile

My New Family
Brad, Me, Kristina, Johnathan, and Eva
Johnathan's Wedding
Summer 2010

Has it been easy? *No!*
Has it been worth it? *Yes!*
Life is a total adventurer
Never a dull moment.
Thank you, God, for saving Brad for me and not
Letting some other woman sink her hooks into him.

He knows the plans
He has for me,
Plans to prosper me,
Plans for good,
Plans not for evil,
Plans to give me
Hope and a future.
(Jer. 29:10-12)

What's Important

Like I said, God knows that my heart, purpose, and passion in wrttin' are to be a voice for hurtin' kids. I didn't say things to be dishonorin' to anyone, but more to have others understand what's happened to me. I believe inside us all is this need to be heard, and since this story is only mine, I can tell it if I want to! *And I want to!* Did I leave out some of the dirt on me? Well sure! Wouldn't you if you wrote a book about yourself?

See, I know He ain't through with me 'cause He's still workin' to make me what I ought'a be. Still, I'm glad for the chance, right now, to write my story and say, "*Thank You, God!*"

I've always been grateful ever' since kneelin' in those shavin's for the encouragement from others and 'specially for the words of my favorite hymn, "Farther On". The last verse has carried me through so much:

"As I travel through the desert, storms beset us by the way.

But beyond the river Jordan, lies a field of endless day.

Farther On, still go farther. Count the milestones one by one.

Jesus will forsake you never. It is better *Farther On*"

God bless you, dear reader, and thank you for your time.

ABOUT SANDY FAULKNER

Qualified?
No, unless English Comp 101 counts. Privileged? Yes, to have been forever touched by stories of triumph: Books—*The Hiding Place, Same Kind of Different as Me, The Book of Job;* Movies—*Facing the Giants, Courageous, and Shadowland.* It's Sandy's passion to focus attention toward everyone's potential to be either a contributor or contaminator in relationships (a "Dr. Phil-ism"). The works listed plus Karen's story, *Farther On,* motivate anyone with faith in God and sensitivity to others to *never* underestimate the gift of advocacy.

An Unlikely Beginning:
Winter of 2011—Trembling and crying Karen gives her testimony discovering she and Sandy share common passions and purposes: intervening for "hurtin" people. A suggestion to record her story leads to Karen's 53,000 word story, whispered on a Wal-Mart Dictaphone, arriving in Sandy's mailbox one month later. Sitting in 12 D Sandy listens and types trying to control her crying, laughing, and gasping responses to Karen's story; so, it is no surprise the passenger in 12 C asks, "what *ARE* you listening to?" Glimpses into Karen's faith, humor, determination and grateful heart, make Sandy's first book writing experience and entire flight a joy. Coming to know Karen as a friend starts and remains an ongoing blessing!

Sandy works in Texas as a Nutritionist in cardiology prevention with her husband, Dale. Courses in Christian Counseling, Bible

Studies, and the Ministry of Houston's First Baptist Church confirm opportunities to encourage others. If writing or having Karen publically present her story moves even one person to faith or motivates others to advocacy, this effort is already eternally valuable.

A Thank You by Sandy Faulkner

Writing *Farther On* would not have been possible without Karen Gryder, family, friends, and the members of His Glory Sunday School Class at Houston's First Baptist Church. Karen's trust and patience made each call and email unstressed, like talking with a friend. At times of doubt, friends like Beth Voss and Peggy Nolan shared the vision and challenged insecurities. Church class members supported with prayers and comments. Dale as husband and best supporter, sacrificed 15 pounds as typing replaced cooking; also, each child (Emily, Amy and David) proofed, edited, encouraged and, when visiting, ate a lot of pizza. I am grateful!